MONEY& POWER:
Thoughts and Notes

By

James A. Hall

HARLEM BOOKS

DEDICATION

I dedicate this book to all people of the earth who stand in the gap in the war against racism, poverty, political corruption, cuts in education, sexual discrimination, the war on drugs, mass incardination, cuts in health care, corporate destruction the environment, the theft of our civil liberties, and global domination by corporations in their BLIND WILL TO POWER.

Let the Circle be Unbroken

"The mind, once stretched by a new idea, never returns to its original dimensions."

-Ralph Waldo Emerson—

ACKNOWLEDGMENTS

My heartfelt thanks to all those great thinkers, warriors and peace-makers who blazed a trail for me to follow. Because of them, I have no excuse but to add my voice to the chorus, my blood and bones to the struggle. All praises to the Most High.

INTRODUCTION

"We can have democracy in this country, or we can have great wealth concentrated in the hands of a few, but we can't have both."

Louis D. Brandeis

On the surface America is a nation of wealthy people, the envy of the world. The nation is often compared to Ancient Rome at the height of its imperial power. American households command the aggregate sum of $16.6 trillion, financial institutions $24 trillion, commercial enterprises $21.3 trillion, S&L's $7trillion, life insurance companies $4.3 trillion, and tax-exempt foundations and universities another $7.6 trillion.

However, a closer inspection reveals that the top 20% of US households own more than 84% of the nation's wealth, and the bottom 40% combine for a paltry 0.3%. The top 3% held 54.4% of all wealth in 2013, up from 44.8% in 1989. The bottom 90% held 24.7% of wealth last year, down from 33.2% in 1989. To drive home the point, the Walton family (majority stock holders of Wal-Mart) has more wealth than 42% of American families <u>combined</u>.

In contrast the nation's wealthiest households, two-thirds of American families earn less than $30,000 a year and are often in crisis mode when the bills come due. The income gap is widening at such a rate that it has become a danger to the level education, amount of health care coverage, national income growth, our democracy, life expectancy, individual happiness and more...

And, in the light this decline in the quality of life of America's working class, corporate entities mobilize their considerable financial resources to oppose: a national increase in the minimum wage, a government assisted reduction in the cost of higher education, a national jobs bill, heath care reform, federal policies that will help to reverse the flow of American jobs overseas, and income equality for women legislation. All of which have the support of the majority of Americans.

The conservatives (corporate cronies) argue that there is no money, that the nation is up to its ears in debt (at last count $19 trillion). So, I suppose they have a point.

But, oh wait. There's money for expanding the budget of the military industrial complex, for waging wars in Syria, Iraq, and Afghanistan. There's money enough to provide the wealthiest Americans with hefty tax breaks. Even with our multi-trillion dollar liability, we can still afford to subsidized corporations like Exxon even as the world's second largest corporation registers record quarterly profits.

Is it any wonder that a self-confessed socialist, Bernie Sanders, is attracting the largest crowds of any candidate as he campaigns for the democratic nomination for president? How long before the American people are so fed up with our do-nothing congress that they rise up. We saw glimpses of America's growing outrage during the Occupy Wall Street protest.

And, still the powers that be refuse to listen. That's because it isn't one man or group of elite that protects the status quo. The capitalist system, which most belief is above reproach, protects itself. But, the capitalist system itself is beginning to be called into question by the masses. The most glaring criticisms are:

<u>Capitalism leads to underutilization of productive capacity</u>: America annually operates at about 79% industrial capacity. Consider the government's refusal to upgrade the nation's faltering infrastructure, to support R&D think tanks, or to provide every American who wants to go to college with the opportunity to do so.

<u>Permanent sectors of unemployment</u>: The

unemployed can be used to frighten those employed into accepting slave wages. The result is a manipulation of the labor market by the capitalist class.

<u>Periodic crisis related to the market economy</u>: In the words of Gordon Gekko, from the motion picture *Money never sleeps*. "The mother of all evil is speculation." Recall the recent market crisis precipitate by over speculation in the housing market. Need I say more?

<u>Waste associated with advertising, legalized lies.</u> The cost of brainwashing the masses into confusing their needs with their wants is enormous. An ad during the Super Bowl can cost up to $8million for a 60 second spot. I wonder what the cost of a pair of Nike sneakers would cost if the company wasn't spending billions to <u>convince inner city kids that they can't life without them.</u>

<u>Incredible poverty in the mist of wealth caused by a structural shift of America's economy from manufacturing to white collar and service industries:</u> Tens of millions of Americans without the <u>skills</u> or <u>education</u> to compete (in the global market place). And as a result, they are permanently locked outside the American mainstream (the American dream).

Racism and human exploitation practiced on a planetary scale: It is carried out by a neo-colonialist system, which is implemented by such "respectable" organizations as the World Bank, the Federal Reserve the IMF, and the Rockefeller Foundation, and a long list of others. Inequality has run so out of control, that the 85 richest people on the planet own the wealth of half the world's population.

It's all about money and power. And, this book is dedicated to revealing the powers (secret societies) at work behind the scenes, the abuses of power by our politicians, the growing concentration of wealth in America, and how the oligarchs have succeeded at turning America into a nation of monetary slaves.

1 ALL CONSPIRACY THEORIES ARE NOT JUST THEORY

All conspiracy theories are not just theory. Are there dark forces pulling the strings of government from behind closed doors? Are the Illuminati, Bilderberg, and the Freemasons what some are saying they are. Perhaps, perhaps not. This book will provide some facts to help you make up your own mind.

Is the White House for sale? For that matter is America up for sale. There is so much money involved in politics today how can the government be expected to look after the people's interest. And, yes, we are allowed to vote. But how free is our choice. Even with an actual choice, a recent decision by the Supreme Court (Citizen United ruling) permits the voice of the people to be drowned out by massive corporate spending.

Naturally, big businesses only bankrolls politicians who protect their interest. It would be illogical for them to do otherwise. Similarly, it would also be illogically for politicians to change a system that puts them in power.

So, that begs the question: what kind of democracy do we really have? The answer is: America is a polyarchy, a term introduced by Robert A. Dahl. According to Dahl, power resides in the hands of elitist sectors of the nation's wealthy. Truth is, real power is exercised by the elite and always has been.

At the heart of democracy is the belief that we are all born equal. And that equality must be accepted by those in power. In an effort to secure that right, many have been tortured and killed as those in power fight to deny it. Recall the woman's rights movement, the civil rights movement or the more recent occupy Wall Street movement. Those who champion democratic ideals are called extremist and labeled trouble makers. So, it is safe to conclude that no one in power really wants a truly democratic system. Amongst those elite sectors protecting the status quo are the corporations.

Corporations

Government has to balance the needs of the whole society, including that of corporations, along the lines of ethical, social and moral responsibility. And, in the discussion of corporations, they are considered individuals with all the rights guaranteed by the 14th Amendment (which ironically granted freedom to slaves after the Civil War).

The corporation is an artificial creation that has twisted the 14th Amendment to mean that they are no different than any other American citizen. But, corporations, in fact, are not people. They do not feel. To them all that matters is their bottom line. Like the unfeeling and greedy entities that they are, their only aim is to gobble up as much profit as possible. You see, by law they must put the welfare of their stockholders above all else even the public good.

This is a very conscious legal decision. Short-term profits for their stockholders, who are very concentrated, are put above all else. Read about the battles between food and health watchdogs and chemical corporations over whether to allow antibiotics in our food supply. Follow the history of drilling and fracking in the U.S. where corporations pursue profits at the cost of decimating the nation's farmlands and underground water supply. And, when you examine the repercussions of these types of corporate victories, you will begin to realize the level of crisis we're at in this country.

And when they can't win in the courts, on the House floor, or through regulatory agencies, they cheat. Whether corporations obey the law is determined by whether it is cost effective to do so. Regulatory fines and penalties are but slaps on the wrist compared with what they stand to gain. Again, the bottom line is all that matters.

For example, Wells Fargo and JP Morgan Chase were recently fined 24 million dollars for their part in a mortgage kickback scheme. But, the fine came only after they had pocketed hundreds of millions.

<u>Corporations are global entities and governments don't have the power they once had over them.</u> Governments are powerless by comparison with the influence they once enjoyed just thirty years ago. In order for corporations to expand their profits they must sell more products and thus consume more resources.

Look at the ecological apathy that goes into such a policy. The result is rising environmental pollution, sprawling industrialization, and corporate expansion into foreign countries resulting in the perpetuation of war and global conflict. We will examine that issue in due time.

Banks

"Give a man a gun and he can rob a bank;
give a man a bank and he can rob the world."

For now, let's turn our attention to a different type of corporation, the Federal Reserve. Gold is only valuable because it is scarce. The same holds true for currency. <u>The more money in circulation the less valuable it becomes</u>. The Federal Reserve has the power to control the amount of money in circulation.

You would think that the power to control money would be in the hands of the government. Surprisingly, the Fed is neither a component of the federal government nor any other level of government. So much for public accountability.

In reality the Federal Reserve is a cartel, a collaboration of privately owned banks. No different than the oil cartel. So, we know what they are, just not who they are. Don't believe me, name one. Ok, so you named Chairperson, Janet Yellen. Very good! Name another? I thought so.

According to Benjamin Disraeli, *The world is governed by different personages from what is imagined by those who are not behind the scenes.*

"The one aim of these financiers is world control by the creation of inextinguishable debt" warns Henry Ford.

"...a power so subtle, so organized, so complete and pervasive they better not speak above their breath when they speak in condemnation of it," wrote Woodrow Wilson.

The banks comprising the Fed have a monopoly, meeting behind closes and interacting with corporate and government entities around the globe. Nothing wrong with that except that the American people are only privy to what they tell us. Examine the outcome of the present fiscal arrangement.

Isn't it odd that wages never keep up with corporate profit? Thus, more Americans are living from paycheck to paycheck in a constant struggle to survive and in constant fear that the market trends and vicissitudes will cause them to lose their financial footing and plummet down into a hellish poverty. This treadmill of the powerless is a direct result of the present system of finances, where banks and corporations wheel enormous power over our daily lives.

In essence, here's how it works. Every dollar the government borrows from the Fed it has to pay back with interest. All of our income taxes are used to pay off the debt that the government accrues. This is all a matter of public record and easily variable should you care to look. Even the founding fathers tried to steer clear of a central bank, what they saw as a perilous road. <u>They understood that debt was another form of slavery, one irrespective of skin color.</u>

But, after a history of failed attempts by other bankers, J.P. Morgan succeeded. He and others of a short list of banker kings caused the market panic of 1907. The collapse was of such proportion that J.P. Morgan was able to sell the public on the need for a central bank so such a panic would never happen again. In 1910, on Jekyll Island, a Morgan property off the coast of Georgia, they signed their Faustian-like pact.

The meeting was so secret, so concealed from government and public knowledge that those in attendance disguised the names in route to the island. It was there that finishing touches were added to a document that give birth to the Fed, the most gigantic trust (monopoly) on earth.

President Wilson went along to gain the presidency, a move he would soon regret. Faced with a crisis of conscious, Wilson went on record against the new lords of Wall Street. Banks drastically increased the money supply, making million of new loans, until the market crash in 1929.

In the aftermath of the worst financial crisis in American history, major banks bought up faltering banks and corporations for pennies on the dollar. Banking power in American becomes absolute, even over other sections of the power elite (C. Wright Mills).

Now jettison forward to the crisis in the financial markets of 2008. It was called a bailout, but in reality it was the largest unregulated transfer of wealth in human history-that is until President Obama's 700 billion bailout of Wall Street in2008. The United States treasury (headed by Henry Paulson formerly of Goodman Sachs) turned over, with the consent of Congress and the White House, 700 billion dollars to the nation's most powerful financial institutions.

The leverage that they used was that they

(the banks) were <u>too big to fail</u>. In sum, whether in the housing markets, hedge funds or derivatives, the American tax payers will be there to cover the losses. But, record bonuses, golden parachutes, and stock options belong only to the titans of Wall Street. *In God we truth* may by inscribed on our dollar bill, but it should read *in Greed we truth*.

The Media

The media in America is owned by the corporations. So, how well can we trust what they report? If we make our decisions and formulate our ideas on the information provided by the media, then everything we think is suspect. If you watch even not-so-closely you will notice how the media keeps the discussion within the narrow margins of approved boundaries.

This allows them the media to present both sides of an issue, giving the impression that we have a democracy. But, whatever message big business wants carried forth in their reporting, what slant the corporations want presented, the media will carry it out unfailingly.

I know some of you doubt that this is the case. If what I say is true, the media would need the capacity to convince millions of American to routinely vote, act, and embrace that which is in opposition to their own political, economic, ecological, and social interest.

And, the media is able to accomplish this through the manufactured consent of the America people. Manufacturing consent is a term from Walter Lippmann's *Public Opinion*. He called it "a revolution in the practice of democracy, a technique of control." He believed that governance is the domain of a specialized class, necessary because the public is not up to the task. "<u>Necessary illusion is required because the average man isn't rational, relying instead on faith and emotion</u>. "

But, America's rule class is faced with a problem according to Lippmann. When the state can't rule by force and people have a will and a voice, how can the ruling elite exercise dominance? But, Lippmann had the solution. They have to control what people think. Freud said that: "man was forever incapable of governing himself thus in need of control". For that reason we would be forever discontent.

A nephew of Sigmund Freud, Eddie Bernays, developed the science of public relations, how to curry favor with the public. He perceived the public as a mob, containing too much irrational energy. After conducting extensive studies, he concluded that in order to control the mod you have to play to its irrational emotions. He took his clues from the way people could be conditioned to dress the same while they remain deeply unique by nature. The psychology of dress was a key example of what was possible.

The advertising industry learned to sell to people's emotions and not their intellect. They mastered the art of making people believe that they needed a new product by building an emotional bridge from the product to the consumer.

Fundamentally, people have an unrecognized longing that can be tapped into using various psychological techniques, placing Madison Avenue in the control of our deepest desires and primordial fears. Mass mind control could be used to manage the *bewildered herd* is how Bernays put it. By manipulating the internal wheel and cogs of the mass mind, they were able to alter the power relationship that had existed since time began.

George Orwell, in his brilliant novel *1984*, maintained the possibility of a perpetual ruling class.

One of the key ingredients would be a perpetual war. In that sense, the war with the terrorist is the perfect war. The enemy (Isis) is everywhere and nowhere at once. More importantly, they are in endless supply.

Orwell and Bernays both concluded that by triggering needs and desires you can get people to do what you want them to do. Getting people to focus on what they want and not on what they need. Appealing to the masses requires linking the product to people's desires. So, by pushing the right buttons, one can sell the people anything from toothpaste to warfare.

War and Propaganda

Remember how not-so-long ago the American people were conned into going to war under the pretense of locating and dismantling WMDs. The Iraq War led to billions in profit for the military industrial complex. With big business in control of the White House and the media and Congress asking all the wrong questions (beholden to the military complex), look what was possible. Notice how both the media and Congress were repeating the lines spun by the White House, over and over and over again.

"...but we don't want the smoking gun to be a mushroom cloud," to quote Condoleezza Rice.

Remember that unforgettable tidbit from the White House's campaign of fear? Remember that? In order to pull off the con, they needed to fabricate a nemesis, one we could properly hate and fear. Enter the Arab world. Early on the spin doctors began associating the Oklahoma booming to the Middle East, repeating the deceptive lines of the government in around the clock sound bites. <u>The human side of the Arab world was hardly reported</u>. Instead the Islamic world was discredited and labeled foreign devils and a threat to the west.

The ministry of information or the White House Press Corp. did their jobs exceptionally well. But then, so did the media. Hundreds of thousands of dollars were spent on sets (with all its hi-tech imagery) used to report the war. The American people were not only expected to support the war, but to enjoy it as well.

The selling of the news (and thus the framing of the truth) meant training news people to say certain things a certain way. The media excelled at distorting the truth and crafting a lie in its place. There credo being: *a lie is as good as the truth if people believe it.*

After the WMD lie was exposed, they went right to work selling the story line of liberating the people of Iraq from Saddam Hussein. What was really at stake was the geo-political value of Iraq and, of course, the region's oil supply.

The pretext of weapons of mass destruction was to control an important part of the world. It's as simple as that. In the process, the values and principles of our Constitution were revoked, placing the power to make war in the hands of the few instead of the hands of the many, the way it was intended.

The campaign of fear and hatred resulted in the lost of certain basic freedoms in the creation of Homeland Security Agency and the enactment of the Patriot Act. American can now be jailed or spied on without respect for due process (4th Amendment). The enemy is everywhere, remember. Thus, every American is a suspect.

Consequently, the greatest casualty of this war has been our basic freedoms, resulting in the silencing of voices of descent and the growing intolerance of opposing ideas. Neo-conservatives or hawks (as they are sometimes calls) are trying to render the nation to a place beyond good and evil, were we are alone and above international reproach. *It doesn't matter that they like us, only that they fear us.* This reasoning, or lack thereof, brings to mind Imperial Rome in her reclining years.

And, always at the heart of their attack is their effort to spread fear. The terms "Axis of Evil" and "radical Islam" is another example of the politics of fear. This type of politics is far more dangerous than the terrorist themselves. Remember all of the color (red, yellow, and orange) alerts that we had to suffer through?

The enemy are going to attack from "somewhere" said the government, but the when, where and how they didn't know. Other than to heighten fear among Americans, what good did it do? When the President was asked what can we the people do to help prevent attacks against our nation, he told the people to *just go shopping.* Be good little consumers, and we'll handle it. In addition to the death and destruction and the loss of our precious civil liberties and a loss of faith in our government, the two wars have nearly bankrupted this country.

The Future

It would be disingenuous to promote the idea that corporation don't help sustain our privileged lifestyle. But, what price are we willing to pay for what they give us. So, will people continue to bury their heads in the sand? By not looking at the problems facing this nation directly, they don't appear to be all that bad. Few squawked when the government started putting electronic tracking devices in American passports. Some Americans have even volunteered to have government transmitters implanted into their anatomies. Can you say BIG BROTHER?

"We shall have a world government whether we like it or not. The only question is whether It will be by conquest or consent", Paul Warburg council on Foreign Relations assures us.

One thing is for sure, there will be a long list of crisis for which big business, through a purchased political clout and a submissive media, will be able to manipulate. An ever increasing number of planetary crises will provide the grist for the mill of the Hegelian Dialectic.

"What we think we see is often an illusion

intentionally presented, like the conjuror who would have you believe he holds a marble in his right hand, when it is actually in his left hand. Citizens of the world, whether their sympathies are left-wing or right-wing, monarchist or republican, have been used as pawns in their game of Hegelian psychology by the hidden hand that rules."

With the world's fossil fuel supply growing dangerously low, gas prices are sure to continue to rise. Food prices will follow suit along with most other household commodities. Considering that the world's population has reached the 7 billon mark and doubling every 35 years, there are troubling times ahead.

Our present course is unsustainable. But, just what does that mean?

Our government will, in the face of such problems as energy insufficiency, pollution, crime and mass incarcerations, widening poverty, war, lost of civil liberties, growing homelessness, systemic corruption and economic disparity, grow even more ineffectual.

But we can win back out democratic freedoms, save our environment, and put an end to hawkish ambitions of the military industrial complex. But, we have to first stop being obedient little consumers trying to buy our way to freedom. The dollar *is* all powerful.

Therefore, we can no longer afford to keep giving corporations our money so they can turn around and undermine our democracy. <u>We have to begin doing business with companies that do business in a socially responsible way.</u>

We have to stop allowing the advertisement industry from telling us what to buy with our money (power). Right choices about everyday decisions can change this country. Corporations, no matter how powerful, cannot survive without us. Don't underestimate the power of your purchases. Deny big business their profits and they will change their destructive practices. And, we can start by demanding the facts and then by acting on that information.

2 MONETARY SLAVERY

The world is controlled by a consortium of institutions (political, social class, occupation specialties, religious, financial, and economic). But, the monetary institutions (systems) are the most powerful. <u>Those who make the gold, make the rules.</u> Few people stop to consider, how money is created, the policies by which it is governed, or its effects on society.

The life blood of all institutions is money. Understanding money is critical to understanding why our lives are this way. The global monetary system is a socially paralyzing, an repressive apparatus that's exploitative in nature. How else can you explain the growing income disparity in the U.S.?

The top 1% owns about 40% of the wealth in the U.S. The top 20% of the population owns the vast majority of wealth while the middle class and the poor are left with nearly nothing.

Specifically, the upper class is growing while the middle class is shrinking. And, the poor are receiving less aid in the daily struggle will hunger, poverty and illness. The income inequality in American has grown obscene and even criminal argues Senator Bernie Sanders.

Still, most Americans cling to the notion that they are better off than those in "developing nations". They reason that life in the devil's paradise is still paradise. They would argue that our wealth has afforded us a way of life parallel to none. And, on the surface, their view appears accurate.

However, "None are more hopelessly enslaved as those who falsely belief that they are free." Keep this in mind as you continue reading. So, if money is freedom consider how it (money and thus freedom) is created.

Creation of Money

Let's say that the government decides that it needs 10 billion dollars.

1. The Department of the Treasury notifies the Federal Reserved that it needs 10 billion dollars, and they prints the equivalent amount in treasury bonds. The action on the part of the treasury prompts the Fed to prints 10 billion in Federal Reserve notes (cash). The truth is, money is created electronically, but for the sake of this simple model we'll use cash. Only 3% of

America's wealth is in the form of currency. 97% of the wealth is in computers.

The bonds (promissory notes) are then swapped for the Federal Reserve notes (cash). The money is then deposited in a commercial bank, adding 10 billion dollars to the money supply. As most of you know, commercial banks are obligated by law to maintain about <u>10%</u> of that on deposit on hand(required reserves).

1.   This leaves 9 billion in excessive reserves. Thus, 9 billion is created out thin air, if there are demands for loans. <u>And, here we thought that only God can create something of value out of nothing.</u> This same process can be repeated 9 times, resulting in 90 billion created from the original 10 billion dollars. The process is known as <u>fractional reserve banking</u>.

The fractional reserve banking system gives value to the new money and steals value from the old. I use the word steal because the money supply is increased regardless of the demand for goods and services. Because of the supply/demand equilibrium, prices tend to rise causing INFLATION, thus debasing the value of money, resulting in a hidden tax on the American public. Since the creation of the Federal

Reserve, the American dollar has lost <u>94% of its value.</u>

So, this process of money creation assures perpetual debt for Americans.

For that reason, money is debt and debt is money. So, if the U.S. government paid off all of its debts, it would lose the power to create money out of thin air. And, while, the principle amount may be paid off in time, the interest accrued cannot be repaid unless more bonds are sold and more debt acquired.

Thus, debt is built into the system; resulting in the America's working class getting the short end of the stick. Wealth is the transfer of debt on to the backs on those already overburdened with debt.

Those who cry foul and point out that the game is rigged are accused of failing to read the fine print. Those foreclosure victims who take legal action (contesting the legality of the contract agreement) quickly find themselves bogged down and mired in legation that may last for decades.

Most Americans are laborers and capital controls labor by controlling wages. This can be done by controlling money (supply). So, in reality, the present monetary system is a modern form of slavery.

Because money can only be created by government liability and (low interest) commercial loans, the American working man/woman must remain on the hamster wheel of indebtedness to assure the survival of the system.

Take the average homeowner for instance. The bank made the loan with money that never existed in the first place. The homeowner then works for 20 or 30 years to pay the loan off. With no more that a wisp of numbers on an electronic ledger, the banker was able to milk a life time of toil and sweat from the so-called borrower. Who said that you can't get something for nothing?

The money only came into existence the second the bank issued the loan and not a fraction of a second before. The banks mathematically predicts-well in advance of the loans- that a certain percentage of the loans will fall into default, leading to bankruptcy and foreclosures. Because of the way that the loans are structured to the free floating financial markets, continued defaults are a certainty.

The <u>dysfunctional and fraudulent</u> nature of the system becomes increasing obvious as one reads the fine print. Like always, the devil is in the details. And, the devil is not without his charms (deception).

The American people have been hoodwinked, bamboozled, run amuck. We are tethered to a system that views us a mere chattel property to be used as they see fit. And, while, we are assured the system is fair and balanced by our leaders in Washington, the entire system edges closer and closer to the edge of the abyss.

3 CORPORATE FEUDALISM

Corporations, governments and the banking systems have devised an ingeniously constructed scam. In essence, it is an invisible war with debt as their primary weapon. Armed with this weapon of mass destruction, they have subjugated American society(and the will of the people).

Once America was under control of this three-headed tyrant, the Corporatocracy set it eyes on the world. According to former president John Adams, there are two ways by which a nation can be conquered. A nation may be subjugated by means of military attack or by economic dependency.

The two primary institutions created for the latter are the International Monetary Fund and the World Bank. Actually, they were created to manage the global economy after WWII. But, when third world leaders began to make noises about freeing their countries from the grip of their economic tyranny (neo-colonialism), the global banks turns their attention to the third world. The bank's combat tactics were simple but extremely effective.

1. Step one. Identify nations with natural resources and arrange for a loan transfer. Preferable

the money should go to large-scale capital projects (infrastructure, power plants, harbor construction, etc). The richest members of the foreign country, the global lending institutions, and international corporations are the primary benefactors.

2. Step two. When a nation is unable to repay the loan, several things can happen. The World Bank or IMF may insist upon equity instead. In example, sell off valuable social or environmental assets (privatization of oil, rice, schools, jails, etc). Other methods of payment may include siding with the United States in U.N. General Assembly votes or contributing troops to one of our on-going military engagements.

3. Step three. What happens when the leaders of these nations refuse to negotiate? Then, they're made an offer that they can't refuse. Labeled as difficult to work with, the nationalistic leader is replaced by a more pragmatic head man (dictator). Consider the rise of the Shah of Iran. When the previous head of state refused to maintain suitable oil prices, he was *persuaded* to leave office. Once installed in office, the Shah killed all reforms and lowered oil prices.

4. (Guatemala 1954) The United Fruit Company

took issue with the land grants (allowed by the privatizing UFC) to the people by president Arbenz. Shortly afterwards, the president was labeled a communist by the CIA and he was taken down in a bloody coup d'état with the U.S. providing planes and military advisors (soldiers).

Then, there was President Aguilera of Ecuador, who stood up to the American oil companies. Aguilera went about reforming the Ecuadorian oil industry so that much of the oil profits went to the people. He was soon assassinated when a mysterious explosive device ripped through his automobile.

Torrijos of Panama was assassinated when he repaid his nation's debt to the U.S. by reorganizing the Panama Canal deal that led to the evidential control of the canal by Panama. A more recent example took place in Venezuela. When the popular former leader, Hugo Chavez, was elected president (in 1998), he pledged to use the nation's enormous oil profits to uplift the people of Venezuela.

When the U.S. banks couldn't bribe him or terminate him, they decided to stage a coup (2002). I use the word stage because the protesters were paid by the CIA and the TV cameras did a great job at editing the footage to make hundreds appear to be thousands. President Chavez would eventually die of a massive heart attack. Some creditable sources believe he was assassinated.

If the economic hit men(those sent in to bribe and corrupt the nation's officials) fail, then the jackals, those with special skills, are dispatched to kill and overthrow. Consider the Iraqi leader, Saddam Hussein. He had been an ally of the U.S. and on the receiving end of U.S. arms. That is until he decided to ignore his orders by raising oil prices, selling Iraqi oil for a currency other than dollars, and by invading neighboring Kuwait.

When that happened, the jackals were assembled (1998 desert storm). Saddam was taught a lesson in loyalty and all was forgiven. In exchange for his life and continued sovereignty, he agreed to allow Halliburton (CEO, Dick Chaney) to rebuild the heavily damaged nation, granting the American-based company billions in Iraqi construction contracts.

Globalization

Globalization is the means by which corporations expand their power to every corner of the planet. As formerly stated, the primary weapon of their takeover is debt, bribery and overthrow.

Once a nation has been infiltrated, the takeover starts with (1) manipulation of a nation's currency by throwing it into a international floating market (2) the cutting of social and educational programs (3) the privatization of public resources (4) liberalizing trade by tearing down trade barriers in order to suppress local businesses and foster unemployment, (5) encourage sweatshop labor to cheapen the cost of labor.

Institutions like the World Bank profess to help emerging nations (economies) out of poverty while increasing poverty and widening the wealth gap.

The Corporatocracy

Some of the most powerful members of this global leviathan are the Federal Reserve, the CIA, the World Bank, Chase JP Morgan, and IMF, amongst others. None of whom are elected or are they held accountable for their life-altering decisions.

Control of the media and political institutions is essential to their nefarious endeavors. Political parties are no more than conduits connecting big money with government. Campaigns are awash with contributions from the corporate and private (corporate channels) sectors. The money required to pay for TV ads only obligate any serious candidate to court the corporate and financial sectors. While pandering to the crowds by day, they reassure corporate American (at ten thousand a plate dinners) of their true intentions by night.

Why does it always seem that a political star (appearing presidential) materializes on the horizon nearly every presidential election? And, who are these people who are chosen to lead our nation. One moment they're corporate heads, the next moment they're heads of state. Consider how easy it was for former president of Halliburton, Dick Chaney, to slither into the White House. Think about what type of president Donald Trump would really make.

Is there any wonder why our political policies are what they are? It should be obvious that our foreign and domestic policies are forged in the caldrons of corporate boardrooms and presented to Congress and the White House by way of think tanks, global foundations, and centers for social, environmental, and political research.

I am not suggesting global conspirators meeting in dark, smoke-filled rooms to plot the enslavement of humanity. Then again, perhaps I am. Regardless, it does seem that U.S. policies consistently help corporate America to maximize profits at the cost of social (human) and environmental (nature) devastation. One has to look no further that the record volumes and profits recorded by the Dow Jones Trade Index in recent months. And, don't give me that trickledown economics bullshit.

Record windfalls (golden parachutes, stock options, and mega-bonuses) are handed out on Wall Street while Main Street is forced to suffer crumbs from the banquet table, forcing it to die a slow and agonizing death. In addition, our politicians consistently promote policies that encourage mounting personal debt, ever-creeping inflation, and growing interest rates.

And, in a world run by corporations (a climate of exploitation and greed); only poverty, sickness and death can flourish. 1% of the earth's population controls 40% of the world's resources. 38,000 children die each day due to poverty and preventable diseases. 50% of the world labors for $2 or less a day. 84 million in the world suffer from malnutrition. 33% of the planet does not have access to clean and affordable water.

4 WALL STREET HAS A GAMBLING PROBLEM

Bulls make money. Bears make money. Pigs? They get slaughtered.

What is the definition of insanity? <u>It's doing the same thing over and over and expecting a different result</u>. By that standard, most of us are insane.

And, OTC derivative speculation is just such an act of insanity that in the end may bring down the American financial system and cause irreparable damage.

Almost <u>every major economic disaster</u> in American history has been due to irresponsible speculation in the financial marketplace. And, at no time in our history has speculation (stock swaps, venture capitalism, hedge funds) been more widespread, or more of a threat to our nation's survival.

At the heart of our most recent economy crisis was the derivative speculation by the nation's largest investment banks. Collectively these financial institutions (driven by greed) delivered the world to the edge of Armageddon.

By definition: <u>A derivative instrument is a contract between two parties that specifies conditions (especially the dates, resulting values of the underlying variables, and notional amounts) under which payments are to be made between the parties involved.</u>

In 1933 the Glass and Stegall Act was enacted, <u>forcing a separation between commercial banking and investment banking.</u> Apparently, lawmakers thought it unwise to continue to allow bankers to indulge in risky speculations with their depositor's money. Not to mention that it was the bankers, <u>dangerously borrowing on the margin</u>, that had just caused the Great Depression.

But, before the ink was dry on the legislation, the banking community undertook plans to rewrite it. That is, failing in their bids to repeal it, they decided to try loosening the restrictions of the law. Mobilizing all the power at their disposal, they convened an army of wingtip warriors armed with Milton Friedman's playbook to wage war against the Keynesians in the name of Adam Smith and all that was holy (laissez faire).

Enter Allen Greenspan, Chairman of the Federal Reserve and advocate of Free Market

Capitalism, in 1993 declared the Glass and Steagall Act obsolete. Corporate banks like now defunct Lehman Brothers, J.P. Morgan, Chase, Goldman Sacks, Merrill Lynch, Bank of American, Citibank, Wells Fargo, and others waged a full-on campaign (employing the most influential lobbyist on Broad Street) to repeal the act.

One writer wrote: "After 12 attempts in 25 years, Congress finally repeals Glass-Steagall, rewarding financial companies for more than 20 years and $300 million worth of lobbying efforts. Supporters hail the change as the long-overdue demise of a Depression Era relic."

The repeal kicked off a marathon of buyouts and mergers, large commercial banks gobbling up smaller investment houses; as well as, titans of Wall Street joining forces in order to better carve up the financial landscape.

By the mid-nineties, the banking elite seemed to have won over even their most diehard skeptics. The Dow Jones was reaching record highs (seemed like every week), helped by go-go stock and the tech boom. The rich got richer and even the middle class saw a modest and momentary uptick in their declining wages. America was once again the land of "milk and honey."

Allen Greenspan, talking his cue from <u>Ayn Rand</u> the hyper-conservative political philosopher, was dubbed the "Wizard of Wall Street." And, the three wise men and Wall Street insiders, Tim Geithner (Treasury Secretary), Larry Summers (Director of the Economic Council), and Robert Ruben(presidential economic advisor and later Treasury Secretary) had President Clinton's full confidence, to put it mildly.

It was around this time that <u>Brooksley Born</u> (close friend of Hillary Clinton) was appointed Chair of the little knows agency, the Commodity Futures and Trade Commission(CFTC). Born was described by her peers as strong willed, yet responsible and accountable. <u>Two traits not usually associated with lawyers.</u>

Not long in office and she directed her staff to begin investigating CDO (Collateralized debt obligations) activity. <u>Plainly put, CDO activity amounts to betting on whether a stock will do well or poorly.</u> Evidently, she uncovered information which lead her believe that there was massive and systemic fraud going on. And, more importantly, CDOs, while yielding astronomical profits for investors, were posing a dangerous risk to the nation's financial sector.

She was soon called on the carpet for her due diligence. She found herself before Allen Greenspan himself. And, while no one knows exactly what was said, it was clear that she was ordered to cease and desist her current investigations into fraudulent activity in the OTC derivatives markets.

 Never mind that dark trades amounted to 27 trillion. Self-regulating, the black box trades or swaps weren't required to record transactions and thus remained non-transparent. As a result, no one, not even Greenspan understood the threat that it posed to the global market's equilibrium.

But, fortunately, Brooksley Born wouldn't back off. This courageous little woman hung onto her convictions like a pit-bull laying claim to a hunk of steak.

I would like to say that this David of the fairer sex took her sling and slue the Goliath. She was even starting to gather believers when Proctor and Gamble filed a law suit against Banker's Trust for swindling them out of millions in a derivative deal. Regrettable, the event only amounted to a speed bump as the banking elite mashed the pedal to the metal.

Pressure was brought to bear and Born was stripped of her power before Congress, but not her dignity nor her certainty about a market crash of crucial proportion in the foreseeable future. Her voice had been silence by those possessed by the blind will to money and power.

We didn't have to wait long for her prediction to materialize. In 1998 LTCM (Long-Term Capital Management) controlled over $100 billion and had positions whose total worth was over 1 trillion. When the hedge fund neared default and approached financial collapse, as a result of its overextension, its spreadsheet revealed a systemic threat.

Turns out that the complexity (inverse trig functions) of the swaps deals were mindboggling, tethering LTCM to dozens of the world's largest banks and funds. Naturally, Greenspan stepped in to bail out the fund and its rich creditors. Thus, a total meltdown of the U.S. economy was averted.

Now the warning signs were clear. But, doing something by way of regulation would interfere with the million dollar bonuses being doled out.

And, the band played on into the next decade. By 2007, the estimated amount of dark trades had reached 595 trillion. Yes, I said trillion.

After the tech bubble burst, the housing bubble proved to be the next cash cow. Sub-prime loans moved faster than a $5 hooker on coupon night and the big boys wanted a stake in the game.

So, billions in housing loans were bundled together into mortgage backed securities. Fannie Mae and Freddy Mac had been the leaders of the housing loan industry. However, when the two giants got embroiled in accounting scandals, they lost their dominance of the mortgage market.

<u>Wall Street then stepped in, using petroleum-dollars and immerging markets monies, to finance the housing loan market.</u> Stringent loan requirements were reduced and sub-prime loans increased mortgage volume. <u>More mortgages, more money</u>. Trillions in loans were handed out on the basis of a stated income (no proof required).

And, while the banking elite knew that the bubble would eventually burst, given the fact that the housing loans were given to people who should have never had them in the first place, they went right on doing business as usual. Most buyers never even understood the terms of the loan or the intricacy of adjustable interest rates.

I had just sold my house, and was renting a townhouse in Virginia during the insanity. I remember waves of different real estate agents knocking on my door daily, guaranteeing that they could put me in the house of my dreams, overnight. It sounded too good to be true.

The whole idea of creating money without creating anything of substance should have sounded too good to be true to America. But, the super banks and global funds continued buying and selling (short sales) the toxic paper. Investment banks continued to put their clients into these iffy securities while reaping huge commissions for themselves.

The formula was the same everywhere and it went something like this: Subprime Loans + Predatory Lending + Target Borrowers = Short Sales Foreclosures

But, it wasn't just the rich; middle-class Americans were selling their home for five times what they paid for it just a couple of years ago. In a year you could double your money by "flipping" it. What

could be more in keeping with the American Dream?

But, like in the children's game of musical chairs, the music finally stopped and the crying began. There were so many corporations holding the valueless securities that lending institutions put a halt to all lending activity in a raw panic. The toxic assets were like landmines, cleverly hidden, with no one knowing there exact whereabouts.

By 2008, Hank Paulson, chairman of the Federal Reserve, was facing systemic collapse, a doomsday scenario unfolding before his eyes. I'm sure the phrase "domino effect" came to mind as one default lead to another and so on.

After gathering the banking elite together, they managed the largest transfer of wealth in the nation's history. And, while it stopped the bleeding, the patient continued to suffer. Millions lost their, homes, pensions, and jobs. And, consequently, their dignity, self-respect, and some even their lives.

And, over a decade later, the suffering continues. I am a Barack Obama supporter, but his choice of financial advisors, Fed Chairman, and Secretary of the Treasury signaled that nothing was going to change. Perhaps, the economy was too weak, to anemic to survive major surgery.

Nonetheless, the fact of the matter remains that Wall Street still has a gambling problem. Even the long since retired "Wizard of Wall Street" admitted to Congress that he was mistaken. Deregulation of derivative was and is a clear and present danger.

Brooksley Born is an American hero, who sacrificed wealth and power in an effort to protect and defend the interest of the American people. Following her conscious, she spoke truth to power. Unfortunately, there are none so blind as those who will not see. She is and was a woman that can be trusted to do the right thing. Those who call themselves public servants could learn a lot from her.

But, there are other brave souls calling for an end to a climate where banks are too big to fail, an end to a self-regulated and secretive derivatives market, and for a start to the criminal prosecution of white collar criminals who rob to get rich.

The last time I looked fraud was a crime, so how did so many bankers, brokers, and managers avoid the federal pen. Instead of going to prison, many were awarded golden parachutes and multimillion dollar bonuses (paid for with tax payer's money), leaving them laughing all the way to the bank. And, the joke is on us, the working class.

So, we are left with a ticking time bomb even after the bomb squad has left the scene.

What did they do in the last Gilded Age? <u>They busted up monopolies; they reined in the oligarchs gone mad, they sent crocks to jail, and they passed tougher securities regulations.</u>

But, instead of learning from the mistakes of the past, big business is calling for more deregulation as a cure-all for the nation's economic woes.

Corporations are people, they claim. They're the <u>job providers</u>, who must be allowed free reign.

They ignore the fact that it was these very same investment corporations that created the worst economic calamity since the Great Depression. And, in less than four years, they had managed, using their same old tactics, to convince million of Americans otherwise.

<u>When President Obama called out Wall Street and offer up sweeping reforms, he was</u>

attacked by the Conservative and abandoned by his own party. It would seem that money talks and you know the rest. And, even before I could complete this rant, the OTC derivatives markets have grown by a billion dollar.

Professor Elizabeth Warren, now U.S. Senator points out: "It is a rigged game that benefits corporations." Like Brooksley Born, Senator Warren has a warning for America. Derivatives are a house of cards. And, we damn sure better listen this time because we may not get another.

5 THE ILLUMINATI

Why are so many people intrigued with the Illuminati? Are they suffering from acute paranoia? Are they just looking for someone or something to blame for their meaningless existence? Is an expanding segment of the American population suffering from a peculiar variety of mentally illness? Do some people just need an explanation for events they don't quite comprehend?

The fact of the matter is millions of Americans are beginning to awaken to the frightening truth. There is a dark force at work behind our present reality. Whether or not you agree with the primary cause of our declining standard of living, you must agree that our daily survival is being threatened. You must also agree that there is something is profoundly wrong. I know that you sense it. Millions have and continue to lose their jobs, their homes, and their life savings. The purchasing power of the mighty American dollar is evaporating like puddles of rain in July.

America is in crisis. And, nowhere is this crisis more evident than in our failing public school systems, soaring divorce rate, the growing rate of teenage suicide and drug use, and the escalating number of rapes and cases of sex molestation.

America has more citizens incarcerated per 100 than any nation on earth. We can't build prisons fast enough.

But, the mounting crisis extends beyond the borders of the U.S. Worldwide; residents of the planet earth are witnessing the spread of terrorism, civil war, famine, ethnic cleansing, disease, arms proliferation, and violations of human rights.

Before offering a historical perspective, let's look at the some immediate and identifiable events in recent history. I asked only that you keep an open mind. First off, was hurricane Katrina manufactured by the Illuminati? It was most certainly not. But, was the response, or lack thereof, a result of the Illuminati's global maneuvering? You be the judge.

While the entire world watched, the city of New Orleans was left to descend into complete and utter chaos. For five days following the collapse of the levies, American New Orleans residents were abandoned by the federal government. No water, no food, no electrical power, and no infrastructure. The only law remaining after the storm was the law of the jungle. President Bush pretended not to know of the crisis. Secretary of State, Condoleezza Rice, shopped for shoes while the 23rd largest city languished in a watery hell.

While the head of FEMA became the fall guy, ultimately it was the president's responsibility. Now, why would the president turn a blinds eye to the suffering of hundreds of thousands of Americans?

What I am about to say may shock you. But, the president was only following orders. And, his orders came down from the Council on Foreign Relations, the North American governing body of the Illuminati.

The leader of the free world taking orders from a shadowy organization? Admittedly, it sounds farfetched. If I were to suspend all good sense for a moment, what reason could there be for the president ignoring a natural disaster of such magnitude?

First, Bush's orders were to discredit the government. Each crisis that the American government fails to address is another brick removed from the wall of democracy. The world watched as the mass media portrayed the callousness and ineptitude of the world's richest and most powerful nation.

Secondly, and perhaps even more frightening, the government's inactivity was a part of a social experiment to test the reactions of not just the city's desperate residents, but law enforcement and emergency services. The Illuminati wanted to test the breaking limits of a U.S. standard metropolitan statistical area. In sum, the city of New Orleans was converted into a lab with the people of the city used as lab rats.

But, let's move on. By now, everyone in the world has read about, watched on television, or discuss with their friends and neighbors the attack on America on 9/11. Was it the handiwork of the Illuminati? I ask that you to do one thing before deciding. Review the tape of the collapsing World Trade Towers. Run it in slow motion. Examine the footage carefully and you will see the detonation of planted munitions at regulate intervals down the length of both towers.

This counts for its implosion. Keep in mind that the towers were built to withstand the direct hits of multiple 707 airliners. Were the building to collapse due to collisions, they would have tipped over, flattening buildings within a radius of a quarter mile.

Here's another juicy fact to chew on. How could the Saudi Arabian terrorist pilot jumbo jets with only a few lessons on crop-dusters in Florida? I consulted with a family member with twenty year experience as a traffic control expert for the Air Force. According to him, navigating a jumbo airliner directly into the towers is impossible without considerable training and experience. It would be like going from driving a motor scooter with only two speeds to driving a twenty-ton rig with 22 gears.

And, where were the fighter planes under the command of the Northern Air Defense Sectors. Standard operating procedure requires that fighters be dispatched from both the Falmouth AF base in Massachusetts and from the Langley AF base at Hampton, Virginia.

So, why would Bush and his cronies order an attack on his own country and then turn around and label it an act of terrorism? They didn't order it. What they did do; however, was ignore the Intel on Mohammad Atta, the head hijacker, and allow the attacker to carry out his mission. The CIA had most the attackers under close surveillance before hand, but was called off by the White House just days before the attack.

Bush had his orders. And, the good servant of the CFR that he is, he stood down in the advent of the Illuminati-controlled assault on our homeland. The ultimate objective was to launch the appearance of a war on terrorism (in the devastating tradition of the war on poverty and the war on drugs).

Bush, exploiting the fear factor, led the America people by the nose into not one but two wars. Each of these bloody and painful conflicts drained America's coffers rendering the nation deeper into debt and forced the American people surrender still more of their precious civil liberties over to the government (i.e. Patriot Act 1&2).

Now, under the disguise of national security, law-enforcement can arrest anyone suspected of plotting a terrorist act and detain them indefinitely. As a result, the so-called war on terrorism has allowed the Illuminati to suspend the Constitution and grant unlimited powers to its lackeys within the U.S. government.

Another power tool of the Illuminati is the Federal Reserve Bank. Contrary to popular belief, the FRB is not a branch of the government. Instead, the FRB is a privately owned and operated. It is an international bank with a governing board of directors. At its core are 300 of the world's most powerful bankers, it stockholders. It stock is never traded on the market, <u>but passed on down the bloodline.</u>

Those bloodlines includes the Rothschilds (Bank of London), the Warburgs (Bank of Hamburg), Chase (Bank of New York), and Kuhn Loeb (Bank of New York). These are but a few of its key members.

Money is power. That being the case, these elite few hold the keys to the kingdom. They are able, without being elected or appointed, to print money through the U.S. Department of the Treasury. The FRB prints U.S. currency without any cost to them and then loans the money to private citizens (via lending institutions) who in turn pay interest. In essence, it's stealing, resulting in the fleecing the American people of their hard labor.

Now, I've made a lot of seemingly outrageous claims and accusations. Why should you believe any of them? You shouldn't. <u>Because, free men and women are critical thinkers and critical thinkers require proof before they accept any claims as truth.</u> And, free thinkers, not mindless drones led by misinformation, are what this proud nation is going to need if it going to defend itself against the ominous forces that plots its demise.

In the pages ahead, I am going to provide you with the history of our enemies. Maybe afterwards you will embark on a search of your own, one that will either dispel or validate what I am about to tell you.

The Rise of Seth (Satan)

Our journey takes us back the year 30,000 BC. You are at the birthplace of the Nile, the cradle of man or the Garden of Eden if you so prefer. You are among the ancient ones. The Self-Created Spirit gazed across the surface of the eternal waters and saw nothing. From Pure Thought sprang existence and out of His month came the laws and principals that govern creation, and from His Soul sprang the Twa, the earliest man.

The myriad of spiritual and material forms are the outward manifestations of the One. In that sense, all things are divine. And, man, like all of nature, has a divine purpose. Man allows God to experience His own creation. He is God's reflection in the waters.

Life acting upon life, giving birth to the living.

When He breathed life into them (the Twa), they lived, but when He anointed them with awareness and a will, they became like Him. From among them he appointed a king to rule the earth, one soul to guide all the others. To His chief steward, He gave the Book of Covenant, thus, crowning His king. The Book bestowed supernatural powers on the holder, connecting him with all life.

With the King as their spiritual teacher, the Twa grew to possess great powers. For untold years, they lived and took life in the garden of the Most High. Unfortunately, some of them became possessed by that power. Jealousy and envy seeped into the hearts of even the most humble and obedient.

Seth, the King's boyhood friend and strongest of the discontents, led a revolt. Seth filled his follower's minds with thoughts of mortality. To achieve immortality, a small band plotted with Seth to steal the Book of Covenant.

Using the knowledge contained in the Book, the King put down the revolt and cast out Seth and his followers from among them. While good triumphed over evil, paradise had been lost. The toxic blend of hatred and fear had become a malignancy. Evil would remain ever-present, always lurking. In hopes of recapturing what was lost, the Book had to be passed on. A search began for one pure of heart. By now lesser beings had started to people the earth.

The Holy Trinity: Osiris, Isis and Horus (Ausar, Auset, and Heru)

Far to the north, at the source of the Blue Nile, was a paradisiacal valley, home to a simple pastoral people. The land was made rich, made fertile by the mineral deposits of the great waterway. The people of the Nile Valley were led by a wise and unselfish ruler, Osiris. He along with his queen, Isis, saw that all the needs of the people were met. No sacrifice was too great.

The Spirit was strong in this King of the Nile Valley. The Book of Covenant chose Him. With the Book, the King joined the upper and lower Nile. His word became law from the northern delta to the mountains of Ethiopia and beyond.

A mighty kingdom flourished around his noble house, and heaven and earth was joined in a middle kingdom. The Book was kept secret from the people, with a few exceptions. After passing a grueling initiation, lasting for decades, an ethical order was formed to cultivate the minds of the people and employ the Book's sacred teachings for the benefit of all.

The first schools of mysteries, as they were called, were erected to probe the stars and master the use of stone and metal. A complex system of writing (Metu Neter) was developed to store knowledge and to advance Science, Mathematics, Engineering, Philosophy, Religion, Shipbuilding, Agriculture, Law, and the Arts. Life was lived and work was performed in accordance with Ma'at, oneness and harmony with all of existence.

As above, so below.

After years of peace and abundance, Seth reappeared in another form. He soon endeared himself with the great king, earning him a place by his side. After plotting for years, Seth slew Osiris. The land erupted into civil war, with those loyal to the king rallying around the queen. Isis, to prevent Seth from obtaining the Book, divided it into seven chapters and dispatched her closest commanders to the far ends of the civilized world.

The chapters were delivered to the secret lodges of Nubia, Sumer, Egypt, Canaan, the Hindus Kush, and the far Eastern kingdoms. The wisest of the wise, those chaste of heart, guarded its secrets.

Shortly after the death of her husband, Isis gave birth to child, Horus. Horus was the hope of the world. His spirit embodied the soul of his deceased father. In time, he vanquished the enemies of his father and ascended to supreme ruler and high priest of the world's schools of mysteries (and keepers of the mystical flame).

These esoteric orders kept the sacred chapters safe for fifteen hundred years. Even in defeat, Seth's hold on the minds of men continued to grow. Surreptitiously, he erected a secret order of his own called the Brotherhood of the Snake.

The dark order's mission was to recover the Book of Covenant (the word of God) and to bend the will of man and nation to the will of Seth. Planting the seeds of hatred and war, they embarked upon a mission to create a one world government under Seth, who, during the Christian era, came to called Satan.

The New Battleground

During the latter days of the great Egyptian Empire, the priesthood, masters of the mystery school of Egypt, were infiltrated by members of the Brotherhood of the Snake. Their coming brought endless power struggles both within the royal lineages and on the national and provincial levels. To make matters worse, the ancient empire was under constant attack by powerful outside forces, starting with the Hyksos and later the Hittites and Libyans.

The high priest and members of some royal houses fled south to the Nile Valley. There, they were protected by the powerful Nubian and Kushite rulers. For a time, the Nubian kings beat back the barbarian invaders and restored stability to the capital cities of Memphis and Thebes.

But, the power of the Snake held sway from Canaan to the north and as far away as the Indus Valley to the east. Students of the mystical sciences had used their great knowledge to build the temples, monuments, irrigations systems, and pyramids. They were moral men, dedicating their life to service of the royal houses and the advancement of the kingdom.

But with their ranks infiltrated by servants of the dark lord, the Egyptian priesthood gradually turned to the black arts (knowledge of the mystical sciences used for evil). Under their malevolence influence, the entire region became embroiled in never-ending war, spreading strife and famine.

However, from the seeds of Egyptian knowledge (the High Nile Valley Culture), other civilizations like Persia, Crete, Greece and Rome flowered forth. In response, the Brotherhood of the Snake was forced to transform itself, taking on a hydra of different forms.

Thus, history witnessed the rise of the occult beliefs including: the Rosicrucians, the Gnostics, Kabalistic teachings, Alchemy, Neo-Platonism, and numerous occult beliefs.

Yet, the great mystery schools continued to preserve their mystical sciences and initiate those worthy into their sacred mystery lodges. Though there were many gifted initiates, none was more notable than the one who came to be known as the Christ.

His knowledge of the mystical sciences surpassed any who came before or after. He was the Son, embodying the Sprit of Horus. Through there is no evidence to support the claim, it is strongly believed that He, the Christ, was the only initiate, besides Osiris, to read all chapters of the Book of Covenant.

World religions would sprout from the rich soil which was His teachings. By now, Satan and his followers were working to usurp the power of the lodges, using emerging nation states to do his bidding, which included undermining the Gospel of the Christ.

The Knights of Templar

By the Middle Age, Islam and Christianity were waging war for control of the Holy Land, Jerusalem. Christian pilgrims were coming under increasing attack, when 9 knights, who called themselves the Knights of Templar, from the west joined together to make safe the western roads to the Holy Land.

The warrior-priests forged a secret order and uncovered the resting place of many of the sacred relics of the Christian faith. These included: the Spear of Destiny, the Holy Grail, and the Ark of Covenant (thought to be the resting place of the Book. In addition, they uncovered the amassed treasures of a score of ancient kingdoms.

But, it was the early writings of the Apostles that were their greatest discovery, scrolls hidden deep within the Temple on the Mound. The Council at

Nicene had altered the true Gospel of the Christ in order to erect a political empire. Under Emperor Constantine, the Church of Rome became the sole interpreter of the Word, giving them sole ownership of the keys to the kingdom of heaven.

The Knight blackmailed the Catholic Church and his Holiness the Pope. In return for their silence, the Knights of Templar were granted free passage across all borders which allowed them to establish an international banking system which further added to their already untold wealth.

The original Templars may have had the best of intensions. But, two hundred years after its start, the Templars were Satan worshipers, holding secret rites and rituals involving pentagrams and blood offerings.

By 1307, King Philip was tire of living in fear. With the Pope's blessing, he ordered the Knights disbanded. Hunted an every turn, the Templars went underground to avoid prosecution as enemies of the Church.

In going into hiding, many attached themselves to a rather harmless organization known as the Freemason. They were builders of the great cathedrals of Europe. To protect the secrets of their craft, the Freemasons forged veils of secrecy. During the Age of Enlightenment, the Freemason's ranks swelled with scholars and aristocrats as a matter of prestige.

While most of its membership were innocent artisans, noblemen, and fortune seekers; the 33 degree master Freemasons had more nefarious plans in mind, like supplanting the Church and exacting revenge against the lineage of king Philip for its progenitors attack on the Knights of Templar.

In 1789, the Freemasons worked from behind the scene to bring about the French Revolution. The heads of Monarchs rolled as long held political traditions vanished. The act unleashed political and economic forces that they hope to harness in their drive for a one world government.

The Illuminati

The Bavarian Illuminati (enlightened ones) was founded by Adam Weishaupt, a Catholic Priest, in 1747. It should be mentioned that the original Illuminati were moors (African and Arabian), whose knowledge recued Europe from the Dark Age and provided the foundation for the Italian Renaissance.

The Bavarian Illuminati's goal was to bring about a one world government under Lucifer. Members of thirteen of Europe's richest families were actually calling the shots. Weishaupt was in actuality a puppet who carried out the orders of the black nobility that had prospered from generations of collusion with both the Freemasons and the Knights of Templar.

The goals and strategy of the Illuminati were spelled out in the Protocol of the Elders of Zion, a document uncovered by the authorities of the time. The Illuminati tried to shift the blame to the Jews. However, once their plans were exposed, many were rounded up and executed for treason and heresy. But, before, Weishaupt could be taken into custody, he was found murdered. No doubt the black nobility couldn't allow the Catholic priest to be taken in for questioning.

The Rothschild family, the wealthiest bankers in Europe, took over the reins of power. The survivors of the purge fled underground by joining the Freemasons lodged in London.

The Freemans in the United States

Most of the Founding Fathers were initiated

into the St. John's Lodge located in Philadelphia, established by some of the colonial society's brightest minds by order of the Grand Master. Thomas Jefferson, John Adams, Alexander Hamilton, Paul Revere, George Washington and John Marshall would all swear allegiance. With the exception of Alexander Hamilton and Benjamin Franklin, most were cursory members with no true knowledge of it Freemason's sullen intentions.

Benjamin Franklin was initiated into the highest level of the order in a special ceremony in London, where the Dark Priest himself presided over the proceedings. There Franklin was given the instructions for the design of the seal of the United States; the pyramidal motif would reference the origin of the organization with the pyramid indicating the incompleteness of the organizational task, and the all-seeing eyes representing the omniscient of Satan.

Those within the inner circle knew that that the eye atop the pyramid didn't symbolize the God of Abraham, Isaac or Joseph, but omnipresence of the dark order.

Numerology was utilized in the seal's design (and later in the design of nation's capital, and even in the nation's legal tender), conveying a message to those in the know.

The offer to join the secret society (with connections to the heads of Europe) was a nearly irresistible proposition, most weren't aware of the masterful plot to steal what Great Britain, with the world's most powerful army, could not conquer by force.

When Thomas Jefferson and George Washington woke to the reality of the subterfuge and Franklin no longer garnering the same influence he had before the war, the Freemasons put their hopes in Alexander Hamilton.

Under orders, he oversaw the creation of a central bank, one with the power to inflate and deflate the nation's currency. With such power, the Freemasons could gradually siphon off the nation's wealth and render the entire population into slavery.

What the conspirators didn't count on was the vibrancy of the American spirit and its passion for self-governance. The American Revolution unleashed a liberating forces that make it difficult for the alien presence to reverse.

And, with the enormous proceeds from the tobacco trade and other cash crops, the new nation was able to starve off foreclosure. So, the dark order bided its time, becoming a fixture in the halls of power and go-betweens for America's ruling elite and the vaults of Europe.

The War of 1812 was the Freemason's first attempt to destroy the young nation. It was this satanic lot that facilitated the war that drove America deeper into debt with the European lenders.

By the time Andrew Jackson moved into the White House, the secret societies of Europe had completely infiltrated the nation, though they still hadn't wrestled control from the old patriots.

When Jackson realized what was happening, he warned his fellow Americans. He was targeted for assassination for his patriotism. Fortunately for him and an unsuspecting nation, the assassin's guns misfired and Jackson survived the plot on his life.

The Monroe Doctrine, drafted by John Quincy Adams, spoiled the European effort to establish a beachhead in Latin America. Which they planned to used to instigate conflict between the U.S. and it neighbors to the south.

The collaborators became too numerous to mention, but even that wasn't enough. So, the Freemasons decided to revert back to their first and most effective weapon. WAR. Divide and conquer was the strategy. The most polemical issues of the time were slavery and states' rights. They conspirators did their very best to empty the U.S. treasury, so by the time of the firing on Fort Sumter, the coffer of the national government was nearly emptied.

However, Lincoln saw through the charade. The Rothschild's were counting on the North winning, but having to mortgage the future of the nation to bring about victory. Lincoln was fully aware of the international banker's motives.

He warned the American people in speeches, but his voice was soon silenced by John Wilkes Booth, agent of the global money cartel.

The plot to impoverish American through the conflict failed because of the discovery of gold out West, which infused the weak economy with new life.

Nonetheless, the trumped up war cost the over six hundred thousand Americans their lives.

Over the next fifty years, J.P. Morgan and J.D Rockefeller, promoting the Federal Reserve; the latest weapon in their arsenal, helped the black nobility to gain control of the American economy.

Shortly thereafter, the nation was plunged into the worst depression the nation had ever seen. Inflation, failed mortgage, and undervaluing American farmlands allowed the Freemasons to fleece the nation and to rob unborn generations of their rightful inheritance.

The next president to take a stand against America's intractable foe was Woodrow Wilson.

He warned the American Public: "There is a power somewhere so organized, so subtle, so watchful, and so pervasive that they (honest men) better not speak above their breath when they speak in condemnation of it."

Once the dark force had acquired hundreds of America newspapers, freedom of speech became a thing of the past. American was steered into a war with Spain even against President Cleveland's better judgment. Admiral Alfred T. Mahan, commander in the British Royal Navy and sworn protector of the British Crown, embarked, through his influence in the war department, the nation on a course of imperialism.

This assured that the contrived German aggression in Europe would pull the U.S. into two world wars. Between the depression and First World War, America's national debt rose by 600%. In the following decades it would continue to escalate.

Nazi Scientist, who were said to be captured after the fall of the Third Reich, delivered the hydrogen bomb. What was heralded as a unlimited source of energy turned out to be Pandora's Box, rendering forth a weapon of mass destruction.

Instead of liberating the world from, hunger, meaningless toil and suffering, it drew the world into a game of nuclear Russian roulette. The political, military and ideological seeds of Armageddon planted.

6 THE WARNING SIGNS

Critics went on to say that the great nation was paying the price for failing to live up to its obligations to is weak and to its poor as embodied in the spirit of its highest law.

Corporate interests, world banks, prestigious law firms and political institutions like the Trilateral Commission and the Council on Foreign Relations had kidnapped the Constitution and held it for ransom.

PAC (Political Action Committees) and influential lobbyist, laden with gifts and donations, were allowed to erode the system from within, until America no longer possessed the fiber to reverse the pervasive corruption.

They further asserted that America's fate was sealed with the importation of African slaves and the slaughter of the indigenous peoples of the Americas.

She was now reaping the harvest of her own immoral seeds. The debt that she owned for her improvidence, selfishness, wastefulness and greed was being called in on the margin. On scorching winds of outraged, voices warned of impending disaster.

The warning signs were everywhere.

The Hiroshima and Nagasaki bombings, the Korean and Vietnam conflicts, and the Cuban missile crisis should have been enough. The massive and utter failure of American school systems to educate the nation's inner-city youth should have warranted a national emergency.

The growing number of militias denouncing the federal government and advocating genocidal destruction for the enemies of the white race should have been called what it was, *home grown terrorism*. The wholesale spread of drugs, violence, and pornography should have polarized a Christian nation in defense of her mortal soul.

The growing rage and outcries of America's frustrated youth, evidenced in their fascination with the morbid and occult, should have been enough to force her to seriously consider a departure from her present course.

Not even the reverse-industrialization of America, the corporate plundering and takeovers, the declining purchasing power of the dollar or the multi-trillion dollar federal budget deficit couldn't awaken the nation from her coma. A coma perpetuated by 'I

Love Lucy' re-runs, Monday Night Football, and un-reality TV.

To a growing number of her people, America represented the democratic ideal but never the reality. They felt that it only served the powerful while sacrificing the dreams and ambitions of its children to feed its lustful and shameful appetite for global control and domination.

The blood of its native sons spilled on the beaches, in the jungles and over the desserts throughout the world. All in the name of democracy. To bring to the world what she was failing to preserve at home.

Democracy requires an educated and informed electorate for one. The masses were never encouraged to think nor were they informed, instead, they were fed a steady diet of misinformation and propaganda by the corporate controlled media.

Politicians, economist and the press had regularly assured the pubic that this catastrophe could never come about, but it had. And, now that it had, they assured the American people that the worst was over and that the present changes in American laws and government were necessary sacrifices for holding the nation together. However, they were wrong again. The worse was crouching in wait in the tall grass of the not too distant future.

7 WE'RE NOT BROKE

Pundits, politicians and economists insist that America is going broke. But, I beg to differ. Ours is a wealthy nation. There is money in America, if only we would look in the right places. National headlines tell of devastating layoffs and downsizing across the country. With states forced to reduce essential services, American is swiftly losing that which made it the envy of the world.

However, these devastating changes to our economic system and to our social landscape are entirely preventable. If only the multinational corporations would stop being <u>deadbeats and tax cheats</u> and burden their fair share of the load.

For example, General Electric paid zero taxes between the years 2005 and 2010, while amassing over 26 billion dollars in profits. Bank of America paid zero in taxes in 2009 (the year it received a 1 trillion dollar bailout) and earned 4.4 billion in profits. Exxon Mobil, in 2009, received a hefty bailout on the way to a 4 billion dollar profit year. Chevron during the same year posted a profit of 10 billion, yet paid zero taxes.

Since 1961, the total percentage of U. S. federal income tax collected from corporations has been cut in half. It should be crystal clear that one sector of the economy is not paying its share. Over the last three decades, <u>that burden has been shifted to the backs of the middle class and working poor.</u>

Faced with the possibility of economic collapse, we will either continue down the road to default or the corporate sector with have to step up to the plate. However, don't hold your breath.

Multinationals have been getting away with paying less, while critical investments in our future (like healthcare, education, infrastructure, research and development, alternative energy, and jobs creation) have gone ignored.

According to the present tax code, corporations should be taxed at approximately 35% on their U.S. earnings. And, to be fair, it is among the highest rates in the industrialized world. But, before you shed a tear on behave of American multinationals; their effective (actual) rate tells a different story.

For example, NIKE's effective rate in 2010 was 22.7%, J.C. Penny's was 15.4%, Coca Cola paid 6.6%, Verizon manage to avoid paying taxes altogether with a -5.9%,Dupont -11.5%, and Yahoo's effective rate was -9.6%.

All this is made possible because the tax code allows U.S. corporations to shift income out of the country to tax havens around the world. This game is played on a mega scale, denying the U.S. Treasury 170 billion a year in revenue. Small countries (i.e. Bermuda, the Bahamas, the Cayman Islands) lacking in natural resources, become business friendly environments, with laws hospitable to foreign capital.

Contrary to popular opinion, it's not just the unsavory businessmen, drug traffickers, and the super rich who dispatch secret couriers to tax havens with suitcases filled with cash. Fact of the matter is, multinational like Apple, Microsoft, HP, IBM, Pfizer, Eli Lilly and company, and thousands of other tech companies and drug makers, do routine business in such havens.

Take the Cayman Islands for example. In one small bank building there are 18, 857 mailboxes, allowing a nebulous of corporations to claim offices (residences) there. Havens like the Cayman Islands act as way stations. Money passes through these way stations so it doesn't' get taxed in the places where it's earned.

But, only in a political and digital sense is the money there. In reality, the money is safely tucked away in a bank vault (advance encrypted database) in the United States. It's just that simple.

Using international tax rules to shift profits out of the U.S. (a high tax country), to countries like the Netherlands and Ireland (low tax countries) is called Transfer Pricing. None of this is illegal, regrettably.

<u>Yes, Transfer Pricing is legal, but is it right?</u> Slavery, apartheid, and denying women the right to vote were protected by a legal system, but were they right in doing so?

The multinationals, other than a mailbox or small office, have neither sales records nor employees in these havens. That's because fortunes of the multinationals turn on American intellectual know-how, research, and productivity. Given these circumstances, shouldn't the fruits of that labor remain in the U.S?

Consider this example. Forest Laboratories, a powerful pharmaceutical company,   makes the antidepressant, Lexapro. 100% of its sales and work force is located in the good ol' US of A. Yet, the lion share of its profits end up in Bermuda, which has a zero tax rate.

Gaming the System

Here's how they game the system. The pharmacy fills your prescription for Lexapro. A chunk of the sale goes to the pharmacy and another to the drug distributor.

But, the bulk of the sale goes to Forest Laboratory's subsidiary located in Ireland (another tax haven). Because of the tax rate, <u>Forest found it more profitable to manufacture the drug in Ireland then ship it to its parent company in the U.S.</u>

To further reduce the Irish tax rate, the subsidiary (Ireland) pays royalties to another company (<u>a subsidiary of the subsidiary</u>) located in Bermuda. Keep in mind that this multi- billion dollar corporation has only a tiny law office on the beautiful island playground.

In 2009, Viagra played the same shell game with its parent company Pfizer. What it saved in taxes increased its net income by a cool billion. Shifting 100% of its profit off-shore helped them to wow Wall Street and secure a strong stock price.

In 2010, even as the economic recovery stalled and job dried up, corporate profits rose by 39%, reaching <u>1.68 trillion</u>, an all time high. As Americans were losing their homes, their jobs, their health, and even their self respect; corporate America, on the other hand, was surging ahead with record profits. And, the wealth gap widens.

Financial globalization got underway in the 1960s. U.S. companies were just beginning to expand internationally. But, the Vietnam conflict was the real kick start. With so much cash going overseas, the U.S. found itself with a little balance of trade problem.

Enter LBJ, in 1968 the president (and formerly one of the most powerful democrat in the House) sought and got a law that essentially required companies to obtain a permit (passport for their money) before moving cash overseas.

Naturally, the young multinationals fought back in a congressional battle, managing to obtain a compromised agreement. In the bill's final form, companies could keep their money off-shore and avoid paying taxes. But once that money returned to the U.S. it was fair game. In the aftermath of the new law, there was an explosive growth of off-shore banking.

Today, over 50 countries act as havens for

profit obsessed multinationals. So, what we've got now are corporations -earning billions in profits, owning trillions in assets, and eligible for billions more in bailouts- paying zero in taxes.

Bring in the Hired Guns

Everything begins and ends with the U.S. tax code, <u>seventy-two thousand pages of loopholes, vagueness and contradictory tax laws</u>. Here, the multinationals turned to outsiders (hired guns): an army of accountants, lawyers, and lobbyist to navigate the voluminous text, using their arcane knowledge to reduce the effective tax rate of their clients.

But, the power of these lords of the tax codes reaches even further. They not only manipulate the codes, they contribute to it. Often these hired guns in Armani suits are asked to testify before congressional sub-committees of the House, Ways and Means committee, supplying drafted paragraphs which are incorporated directly into the code.

There are even more questionable (unethical) means by which multinationals game the system. The IRS, with its limited resources, is often set back on their heels in trying to make sense of corporate shell games (a multi-layered, multi-national series of transactions).

In a revolving door manner, today's IRS officials later become the senior officials in the very firms they're hired to regulate, a lucrative reward for a job not done.

For example, from 2003 to 2007 Mark Everson, IRS commissioner, dedicated his life to plugging loopholes and demolishing shelters. Two year later he joined the Alliant Group, a consulting corporation, where he took his fight back to the Hill, this time urging congress to minimize tax bills. Talk about a turn around.

Corporations are People Too

When Clinton left office, America had a 200 billion dollar surplus. By the time Obama took office, America had a 1 year deficit of 1 trillion dollars with a projected 12 year deficit of 8 trillion more.

The global war on terrorism proved to be quite costly, and not only in U.S. casualties. The Afghan War cost 443. 5 billion dollars and the Iraq War cost 805.5 billion dollars. Soon after taking office, Obama was under tremendous pressure to sign

800 billion dollars worth of corporate bailouts. <u>Thus, the president's policies, like all the others, are forged by corporations</u>. But, the most devastating lost has been the 2. 4 trillion lost since the Bush tax cuts commenced in 2001.

Now as our nation tries to have a serious discussion about the mounting deficit, the multinational are busy reshaping that discussion. One point consistently championed by the Republican Party is that there will be no tax increases. The party of Lincoln has been hard at work perpetuating the myth that Americans are over-taxed. While the truth is <u>European nations, in the aggregate, are taxed at a much higher percentage rate.</u>

Certainly, no one can deny that on our present course, we are headed for a catastrophic default, one capable of bringing the world to the brink of the apocalypse.

Therefore, budget cuts in the trillions are inescapable. Or at least that what conservatives are yelling from the mountaintop. We must <u>all</u> tighten our belts, they say. Obviously, that doesn't pertain to the multinationals.

In 2011, congress cut the national budget by 38

billion dollars, the largest cut in American history. Furthermore, they're looking to streamline (gut) Social Security and Medicaid, and reduce the nation's investment in infrastructure and human capital.

They argue that they are preserving the America way of life for future generations. Yet, what will our children's future look like if we fail to invest in alternative energy sources, more efficient transport systems, and more reliable dams and levees, restoring our bridges and tunnels, reduce the cost of education, rebuilding roads and highways, R&D (technology banks in support of our industrial base), universal health care and 21st century jobs.

As the multinationals re-imagine America, U.S. cities and counties are facing a budgetary gaps that threaten the very fabric of our society. State and locate authorities are forced to lay off essential service workers like teachers, firemen, and law enforcement.

As a result of our lawmaker's irresponsibility, fewer and fewer young (middle class) Americans can afford a college education, crimes (like rape, murder and robbery) are on the rise, and firehouses are being shutdown resulting in needless fatalities.

Other areas are being slashed to the bone as well. Libraries are closing their doors for good, affordable daycare is becoming a thing of the past, and mental health facilities are forced to turn away those badly in need of treatment. Without these critical investments, the wealthiest nation on earth will soon start to resemble a third world country.

Yet, how is this possible when the 1990s was the most financially profitable decade in American history? For a plausible explanation, perhaps we need to consult the golden rule: "he who has the gold makes the rules".

In 2010, General Electric spent a whooping 39 million on lobbyist, another American record at the time. Spending on lobbyist skyrocketed from 1.4 billion in 1998 to 3.5 billion in 2010. It's no coincidence that we began to witness the systematic decimation of America's middle class roughly during this period.

Ronald Reagan called corporate tax a punitive burden. His Morning in America speech promised Americans that they could have their cake and eat it too. He went on to say that "federal government was not the solution, but the problem."

As the former B-list actor advanced in age, the monumental achievements of the U.S may have slipped from his aging mind. <u>These achievements include: the building of Hoover Dam, creation of the Tennessee Valley Authority, connecting the nation through a vast and ubiquitous interstate highway system, rescuing the nation from the grips of Great Depression, construction of the Panama Canal, the defeat of Fascism, etc.</u>

<u>In 1981, tax revenue was 19.6 % of the GDP (Gross Domestic Product). By 2010, it had dropped to 14. 9.</u> These statistics alone point to the gradual underfunding of the federal government.

Part of the problem stems from the, highly-cultivated misconception that we can thrive as a people without paying more taxes. There no way in hell that this is possible, unless you subscribe to the free lunch school of thought.

The Japanese and Chinese moneylenders have kept their interest rates conveniently low over the past few years to encourage our borrowing. But, have you ever stop to think of what will happen should they raise their rates to say, 10%? Can you say global disaster?

So, we have no option but to raise taxes. And, as the Republicans slash and burn their way through future federal budgets, so will the social rampage of austerity continue. Italy and Greece and Ireland have all traveled down that road. Ask the working class and poor of these nations how that plan is working out.

But, it would seem that the multinationals have become a victim of the own creaion, vis-a-vis Transfer Servicing. While U. S. corporations can borrow from the fed when their U.S. earnings are not enough, they would like to be able to bring home their estimated 1.4 trillion trapped abroad.

As a result, they have been working on a <u>tax free</u> return, a repatriation of their overseas profits.

Politician, bought and paid for by corporations, argue that these repatriated funds would create jobs here in the U.S. In 2004, Bush gave the idea a trial run with the Job Creations Act. The new law amounted to a 1 year amnesty on foreign U.S. corporate profits, <u>the rate reduced from 35% to 5%.</u>

During this time, Pfizer's books reflected a profit of an additional 11 billion over the previous year. But, no additional jobs were created by Pfizer.

In fact, they downsized dozens of laboratories and closed several plants. But, it did drive Pfizer's stock up through the roof, earning executives hundreds of millions in stock options.

And, Pfizer wasn't the exception. Citigroup, Ford, Apple, among others, followed the same disturbing pattern. Even in the light of this, Congress is seriously contemplating a bill that would render all U.S. corporate earnings (present and future) aboard permanently exempt from taxation.

They argued that its necessary if the U.S. is to compete with the world. However, the UK adopted the same policy (100% tax exemption on repatriated profits) in 2010. Yet, the money and jobs continued their exit out of the country, leading to riots in London and other cities.

Permitting the multinationals to shelter their profits has/is having a devastating effect on small business in America. It's nearly impossible for small businesses to compete with these hidden profits and other corporate advantages.

<u>Thus, what we see is a 'Walmarting" of America, with mom and pop enterprises becoming a thing of the past.</u> And, just as disconcerting is the idea

that such events are leaving little room for Americans to pull themselves up by their bootstraps. Ironically, the very same politicians railing about protecting small businesses and the entrepreneurial spirit are supporting tax exemptions for the multinationals.

Multinationals own Congress by way of purchase. Their influence on Capitol Hill has never been more on display. Thanks to the Supreme Court (Citizens United), there's literally no limited to their contributions, throwing open the floodgates of political corruption and fraud.

And, the Democratic are no different than their Republican rivals when it comes to raising money. In 2008, President Obama raised 746 million from PAC's affiliated with corporations. However, with the cost of presidential campaigns reaching the billion dollar mark, 1500 dollar donations wouldn't deliver the Oval Office. Some say that Obama's choice was unavoidable, doing a little bad to do a lot of good. Some people buy it.

IBM's campaign contributions, during the 2008 campaign year, amounted to 532 million dollars, Google 85 million, Motorola 69 million, and Xerox 32 million. Why would these multinationals tender such largess if they didn't expect a return on their investment?

Therefore, it should come as no surprise that legislation that would raises taxes on the 1% are met with stiff opposition in the form of filibusters, pigeonholing, and other obstacles. Politicians that try and advance the cause of equity in taxation, pay the price on Election Day. Suddenly, the candidate that's challenging the foolish incumbent is suddenly flushed with campaign contributions.

Their trucks use our highways, our military protects their overseas investments (acquisition of third world resources), and avalanches of corporate litigations overburdens our court systems and they still refuse pay their fare share. Action must be taken to bring the unethical behavior and corruption to an end! But, remember, power concedes nothing. Thus, if change is to come about, people can't just demand it. They must be willing to fight for it.

"We can either have democracy in this country, or we can have great wealth concentrated in the hands of the few, but we can't, but we can't have both"

8 BLOOD MONEY

The drug heroin had a devastating effect on Harlem, almost as much as the monies generated by its sale. The streets were far colder and more menacing than I ever remembered. Most of my childhood friends were now wantabe gangsters with a kill or be killed mind-sets. Easy <u>money</u> dissolved all memories of past relationships and ended all reveries of our childhood days.

Our lives had been filled with games, but never had the stakes been so high. So, when it came to this new game, no one was to be trusted. Business associations, ones centering on the deadly trade, short-circuited all childhood friendships and any sense of community. As I said, there had always been drugs, but the wholesale distribution had grown to accommodate the skyrocketing street demand.

The scores of strung-out soldiers returning home from Vietnam seemed like a blessing to those seeking immediate escape from their impoverished existence. In no time, heroin was king and cash flowed like <u>water</u> down a mountain.

The last vestiges of innocence were the first casualty of the white plague. No longer boys, my former classmates had become armed combatants prepared to battle to their deaths over cash, territory, and product. Dope had invaded urban America, and Harlem seemed like ground zero.

One look and I could see the change in my former crew, their hearts black as night. It was in their swagger; slow and predatory. It was in the way they sprang into action when business called. And, it was in their willingness to spill blood over the smallest affront to their inflated sense of self-importance.

Harlem was now teeming with parentless and village-less <u>children</u> seeking refuge from their pains in the arms of a white malevolent mother (heroin) and vying for the attention of the very same lily white society that left them scorned and abandoned.

They sprang from gypsy (freelance) cabs proudly displaying their rapacious purchases including boxes of sneakers, trendy threads, and gaudy jewelry. Latent down with bags, they strolled coolly, never missing an opportunity to smugly and proudly flash their wads of blood money.

Death and misfortune invited themselves to dinner, bringing with them a ravenous appetite.

'Fat Stevie' (one of my closest friends) had just been indicted, betrayed by fellow council of seven member, Nicky Barnes, one of the most notorious dope dealers on the entire east coast, appearing on the cover of the New York Times Magazine as Mr. Untouchable.

Johnny Page had been stabbed to death with a pair of scissors while sleeping. Apparently, his live-in girl friend got tired of playing the role of punching bag. 'Joe Bud', a self proclaimed Five-Percenter, was set ablaze with gasoline by some Puerto Ricans when he didn't pay up.

'Spanish Louie' was gun down in broad daylight while shopping on 125th Street by his competition. 'Peter Whack' responded to a call from his sister whose boyfriend was going upside her head. When Peter entered the building, the boyfriend emerged from under the stairs and shot Peter three times in the chest. He was pronounced DOA. Durant was convicted of murder in the 2nd degree and sentenced to 12 years.

When Carlisle moved into the neighborhood, the girls went crazy. He was a pretty boy with light skin, smooth features, hazel eyes, wavy hair, and dimples. When he strolled into Nicky's soda shop, girls (three grades older than Carlisle) fought for a seat next to him.

Carlisle was to sex appeal what 'Fat Stevie' was to money. But, when they pulled his body from the Hudson River, his head was the size of a pumpkin, his face in the newspaper resembling that of Emmitt Till. Word was he too mismanaged his debts. There was a lot of that going around.

'Eldorado George', aka 'Earl the Pearl', got his head blown off by a sawed-off shotgun when he entered his building. His brains splattered over a row of mailboxes. 'Bat' was now a reputed dealer. News had it that he had just been robbed and shot down in public by a trigger-happy gang of stickup kids led by one Ivan Johnson, reputed gunman from the Esplanade Gardens housing complex.

Story had it that Ivan was sticking up numerous dealers in the Polo Grounds projects, formally home to the major league Giants. One of the dealers retaliated. The baby of Ivan's crew was cut down in an ambush. The shooting warranted only a small space in the Daily News. But, barbershop folklore told of the crew drinking the blood of their fallen comrade and pledging deadly retribution.

The rest was history, the start of a murder spree that transformed things forever and made the funeral business the second most lucrative enterprise in Harlem. Finally an aggressive task force, at the U.S Attorney General's behest and President Carter, managed to put together a case against Nicky Barnes using the newly created R.I.C.O statures.

Two years later Nicky, consumed with thoughts of betrayal by his closest associates, began "dropping dines". In exchange for his cooperation, he was placed into a witness protection program. 109 indictments were handed down on the strength of his deposition.

Many of those convicted were the very same boyhood friends of mine. To make things worse, a power vacuum was created by the busts, decentralizing the drug trade in Harlem and touching off dozens of block wars, helping to make New York City the nation's murder capital.

9 TO SIR, WITH LOVE

I have been a teacher for the past twenty odd years and I thought that I would never say this, but I am burnt out. If not burnt out, then certainly my flame is flickering in the winds of change.

The sad part is that when I entered this proud profession, I encountered these warped and frustrated old educators. I listened to them railing against the onslaught of their young charges while shaking their fists and cursing the heavens for their cruel fate.

I promised myself that I would never become them. I would leave long before joining the ranks of these malcontents. I'm reminded of a conversation that I overheard in the main office during my first week on the job:

"These kids aren't bad, John," the veteran teacher alleged, sarcastically. "On the contrary, these young people are our future. One day this nation will be in their hands."

The administrator gave the teacher a long skeptical look. "Well, when that day comes, I hope that I'm dead," responded the vice principal before turning and walking away.

I am <u>happy</u> to report that I haven't sunk to such depths, and most likely never will. However, my idealism has vanished, and my passion is fading fast.

I recognized my calling after viewing "To Sir, With Love" starring Sidney Pottier. In the film, Sidney played Sir, an <u>unemployed</u> civil engineer who took a substitute teaching position in the slums of London's East End. To say that his <u>students</u> were hostile toward him would be like saying that Hitler disliked Jews.

There was the usually age difference, but there was also a racial, class and cultural difference to overcome. Sir was educated and urbane, his social refinement and sophistication ostracizing him even more than his <u>skin color</u>.

But, in the end, he succeeded at winning them over, finally transforming this group of rowdy seniors into a gathering of young adults, fully aware of their unlimited potential. Sir's very presence transformed their dingy, dirty little district into a somewhat cleaner and brighter corner of the world. In the final scene (an English version of the American senior prom) he was honored with song and awarded a token of their gratitude. Swept with emotion, tears ran down my cheeks.

My own <u>start</u> was not that different. I had plans of becoming a city planner. After graduate school, I took the city planner's test. My score was more that respectable. Nonetheless, I was informed that it would be a year before the city began calling up promising applicants. With my Fellowship Award <u>money</u> almost gone, I followed the advice of a teacher friend and applied for and received a sub license.

A star was born. I was a natural. Sir had nothing on me. While as a teacher I was technically flawed, lacking formal <u>training</u>, it may have worked to my favor. I employed the trial and error technique, keeping what worked and discarding all else. Other than insisting that they obey my every command without question, I had no hard, fast rules.

The classroom was my stage. It was there that I performed. I was entertaining, young, educated, and street. Perhaps, most importantly, I was strong enough (physically, mentally, and emotionally) to keep the peace. I never became the sled driver, instead; I opted to become the lead sled dog. So, while I was clearly in charge, I was one of them.

You can guess the rest of the story. When the city finally called me up for an interview, I declined and remained a teacher. After all, who wants to be just another cog in the machine when one can be a star in the night sky?

That was over twenty years ago. Since then I has changed from an optimistic young educator to an increasingly pessimistic middle-aged History teacher. Who or what is the blame for this. Is it the students, the school system, the community at large, or myself that is the cause? I have a hunch that it is all of the above.

I sensed that something had changed within me after viewing the movie "Lean on Me", starring Morgan Freeman. He played Joe Clark, the controversial principal of East Side High located in New Jersey. Principal Clark cleaned out a cesspool of a school by tossing out over 300 of the school's truants, thugs, and drug crazed miscreants.

His philosophy was simple. A certain percentage of students will succeed in spite of the school system's failures and ineptitudes. Another percentage will end up dead, in jail, or impoverished despite the school's best efforts. So, the only ones that ready counted, are those in the middle, those teetering on the fence.

With little or no deterrence, many of those on the fence will come down on the wrong side. However, eliminate the core of the trouble makers and most will come down on the right side. It's as simple as that. The battle was for more than their mind, but their very souls.

While he got positive results, neither the community nor the state approved of his methods. As a result, he got canned. I mention him because I'm a Joe Clark disciple. Every garden needs a gardener to prune and clip and clear away the weeds. Without this careful maintenance, what's beautiful becomes unsightly, and what's filled with life and vitality become stagnant and dead.

Walk into any inner-city public secondary school and you'll be alarmed by the violence, taken aback by the profanity, incensed by the insolence and dejected by the indifference.

But, disruptive students are nothing new. I

myself was a card carrying member of the Vice Lords. However, back then, we thorns in the side of the school system represented a mere 2 percent of the class. By the time I became a teacher that percentage had ballooned to about one third. Now, disruptive behavior is widened to include half of the class. Insubordination now commonplace.

To make matters worse, along comes the federally funded "No Child Left Behind" agenda. Its objective was to bring national accountability to public education. Granted, school systems across the nation were and are failing miserably and are badly in need of reform. Washington reasoned that if it were going to continue to foot the bill, it had a right to call the shots.

I have a ton issues with the NCLB, but the primary one is that it forces schools to play the numbers game. If Johnny doesn't come to school, the school doesn't get x amount of dollars. So, no matter what Johnny does, short of assault, murder, or rape, Johnny is allowed to stay.

Well, there are dozens of Johnnies in every school who warrant long-term vacations for the good of the school and to send an unmistakable message to other would-be Johnnies. Among other things, NCLB ties the hands of administrators and forces teachers to accept chronic disturbances as everyday occurrences.

Also, the "mainstreaming" of special needs students may be a great idea, but when the teacher is overburden with regular students, and is not given the assistants (teacher's aides mandated by the law) the results are often disastrous. Many schools do not have the resources to comply with the law, so they simple ignore it.

As a result, a teacher may have a class of 28 students, which includes 6 special needs students who are reading 4 or 5 years behind the others. These students are not able to keep pace without extensive modifications and often one-on-one instruction. In the end, it's a farce that is costly to all involved, and even criminal in many cases.

In regard to the community, school involvement in most inner-city schools is nearly nonexistent. There are a number of reasons which includes the following: single parent families, parent forced to work two jobs, elderly grandparent forced into parenting roles, etc. For the last 5 years I've seen fewer that 5 percent on parent/teacher night.

And, America spends an astronomical among of money on education, but the results are marginal at best. I look back over my twenty-five years with no regrets, reveling in the loads of joyful moments.

I'm not sure what the future holds for me, but know that it's time to call it quits. It's time to walk away from the profession that I loved for so long. I will take with me all the fond relationships forged in the fiery furnaces of the classroom, including students and peers. The salubrious faces, indelibly etched in my soul, will follow me all the days of my life. Walking away now is one of the hardest things that I've ever had to do. But, if I don't go now, I fear that I will come to loath the very students that I've come to love so very much.

In closing, each and every morning I prayed for God's help in reaching those young minds. And, He was there with me every step of the way. There's no doubt in my mind that He put me exactly where he wanted me to be. That being the case, if my leaving offends Him, I pray for His forgiveness. And, I ask that he direct me to my next big adventure.

10 MY LITTLE JAIL SCHOOL

I once thought that the principle solution to the mounting violence and mediocrity of inner-city schools was the systematic removal of the gangbangers, dealers, and thugs.

'Throw the bastards out', as Joe Clark, the famous Jersey principal, would say. Sacrifices the few so that the many may learn. I admit this was a dangerously simplistic and egalitarian approach. However, twenty odd years of teaching experience supported my conclusion.

Unable to retire do to a crashed economy, I accepted an assignment in a city jail teaching juveniles charged as adults. The name of the school matters little. So let's us just call it the little jail school, most people jokingly do.

Inside, a jail has a spuriously calm surface. While beneath the surface lays a deep sea of physical brutality and emotional slaughter. Neither side of the law is unsullied; both sides are deeply invested in the sanctioned madness.

Like eyes adjusting to a dark room, it takes time to penetrate to the murky depths of this sea of human misery.

I remember first standing in front of the gothic structure that is the oldest subdivision of the massive facility. Ironically, it resembled a medieval church, it windows black with mystery. This combined with its towering stone walls and ubiquitous barbed wire gave my new workplace a frightening appearance.

However, equally unsettling was the maze of corridors, courtyards, and choke points in route to my classroom. The callous and no-nonsense nature of the environment was reflected in the icy cold stares of the uniformed staff and the shackled detainees.

Finally, I arrived at my little schoolhouse, a small network of coupled trailers assembled smack-dab in the middle of a maximum-security adult correctional facility.

The jail houses between four and five thousand detainees. The population includes those held on lesser charges like DWI and shoplifting, as well as, those accused of homicide, robbery and rape.

The night before, I experienced the usual melancholy at watching the last hours of my summer vacation tick away. However, I was also excited about the new school year. I used the synergy of emotion to assemble a few mental notes about my ice breaker.

I never had much use for lesson plans on the first few days, preferring to improvise instead. The hand bell rang and the students filed into my cramped and narrow effigy of a classroom, the cheap wood panel walls displaying laughingly clichéd posters like "Just Say No" and "This is your Brain on drugs".

There I stood, face to face with a classroom of baby face killers, drug dealers, gang bangers, stickup kids, and some with severe emotional disorders.

Strangely, they appeared no different than the thousands of other students that I'd taught from New York to Newport News. It was just another first day of school, and they were just kids.

I leaned against the front my desk, scanning my first period class. My face was as hard as stone; my every movement reflected a quiet self-confidence. My tone was quite formal, yet seasoned with my Harlem upbringing.

I ran down the many criminal endeavors of my youth; as well as, my history of gang involvement, both as a member and a councilor.

I proceeded to expound upon the veiled nature of the Crime "Justice" System and the underlying reality of the "war on drugs".

It worked. I had their attention, without which nothing is possible.

Some members of the staff were a little uncomfortable with the seemingly perfect match between myself and these, so called, menaces to society. Teaching strategies that would have been frowned upon by most school administrators were indispensable assets here. It was imperative that I speak their language.

Unlike most teachers, I spoke their language on so many different levels. Nonetheless, it was as much a learning experience for me as it was for them, if not more. You learn quickly that nothing is free behind bars, everything come with a price.

So, I can't say that I didn't experience some tense moments when the novelty of the new teacher began to fade and banality set in. In the end, I made some adjustments, perhaps concessions would be a better word.

In a month's time, I was offered a teaching assignment afterschool and upstairs on the section where the juveniles are housed. There I got my first sobering glimpse behind some of the pretense, beyond the masquerade to the emotional and physical cruelty that exists in such places.

There are roughly 149 juvenile detainees in this jail inside a jail. Most of which are housed on the unit. Those on protective custody or PC are in held in smaller subsection. Another part of the unit consists of those on disciplinary lockdown and those on intake or processing into the system.

The fluctuating population on "lock" or lockdown is remanded to their cells for 23 hours a day and sometimes more. The stench on the juvenile unit is barely tolerable for regulars and nauseating to visitors.

Throughout the unit, an infestation of rodents scamper up and down the tiers feasting on discarded food, gorging on discarded "sweat" sandwiches or "bricks" as they are also called because of their cement-like texture.

Big-timers, roaches the size of an adult index finger, strut about and can be witnessed carrying off pieces of compost twice their size.

After earning a measure of their trust, which is no easy feat, I began to decipher a peeking order, a power structure, one established by acts of violence and cunning.

Though they be young, they be mighty.

These children of our urban wastelands can be devious, calculating and unrelenting. So, it was no surprise that many excelled at the game of chess and some have read, and practiced daily, the "Art of War" by Sun Tzu.

Gang affiliations also play a major part in establishing the order of things. As with most jail and prisons across American, gangs rule. The Bloods, the Crips, and the Black Gorilla Family or BGF often vie for control of this particular lockup.

New arrivals may be spared a beat down or being placed in protective custody if they are able to verify their street connects to one of these families. The weak or unaffiliated detainees are subject to having their commissary taken, or their meals reduced to the least editable items on their tray.

But, mostly, they are harassed and often put in positions of having to steal, to launch hits against other detainees or to lie to protect the guilty.

Everyone tries to appear hard when they first arrive, but poseurs are quickly weeded out. Some are able to prolong the process by remaining silent and detached. Often, this is the safest strategy. But, all are put to the test in time.

Now, most people would say that they deserve this living hell. Others would argue jails are not supposed to be a playground. They say that it will teach them a lesson that they won't soon forget.

I confess that on the surface, they have a strong argument. But, upon closer examination, the argument neglects some important points. First, these young boys and girls are, according to the

Constitution, innocent until proven guilty. Second, they are children. But, more importantly, most can be saved or diverted from the path that they have mistakenly chosen.

You see, if you treat them like animals, they will learn to behave animalistic. If you cage them away for 23hours a day, with rotten food, and no creative means of channeling their frustration, you will only create monsters.

Whether sentenced to hard time or released, most will eventually return to their neighborhoods. Without meaningful reforms to their systems of beliefs, they will return mentally and emotionally damaged; crazed, sadistic and even suicidal?

The criminal justice system has a choice. They can take serious steps to reform (including psychological counseling, training programs, and residential programs and halfway houses that prepare their return) jail become training ground for future miscreant and thugs.

That brings me to the next question. Who are the real victims in this anyway? No doubt, many of these teenagers have left a trail of tears in their wake. Innocent people have died, and lives have been put asunder.

On the other hand, many of my students are but victims themselves. Most have grown up in a gang infested and crime ridden neighborhoods where they are forced by circumstance to embrace aggression or fall victim to it.

Most attended inner-city schools which are miserably understaffed and poorly funded and a recruiting ground for some of the nation's most dangerous gangs.

Some have dope fiends for parents, whose main concern is where their next fix is coming from. For others the drug trade is a family enterprise, with even grandparents sometimes playing a part.

Like other children, my students are bombarded with images of violence from action movies, rap lyrics, and video games. Unlike other children; however, no one has ever monitored what they watch or even sit down and explain fact from fiction. The majority of them have never had the benefit of an ever-present hand to guide and nurture their social development.

Lost and alone, most have turned to the streets for answers.

Are they not victims of a cold and insensitive society that will spend billions a month on wars and weapons procurement, while constantly cutting programs that might make a difference in the lives of some of our nation's most at-risk youngsters?

Few give a damn about these suspected felons, and wish only that they're locked away somewhere. Fueled by the horrid images on the nightly new, more and more people are crying out for the permanent removal of these useless dregs.

But, society *does* have a use for them. Truth is, my students and thousands like them across America represent billions in federal funding.

With the crumbling of the United States' industrial base and the lost of millions of jobs to foreign countries, the government is hard-pressed to create jobs wherever they can. The survival of the economy and the American way of life depends on it.

While I am not implying that there is some back room conspiracy to use black youths as grist for the jail and prison mills, but bureaucracies (including city agencies and unions) tend to protect their inflated budgets at all cost.

And If matter couldn't get worse, we are starting to see the ominous shadow of "privatization" moving across the heartland. Several Midwestern states have contracted with corporations to take over specific operations, including security. This includes thousands of employees and tens of billions in operating expenses and capital projects.

The state in which I reside allocates close to fifty-thousand dollars a year to keep each youthful juvenile offender behind bars, while spending only a fraction of that amount to educate them while in public school.

So where does all of that money go? It goes to paying the salaries of correction officers, probations officers, case workers, judges, magistrates, teachers, principals, and support staff of every kind.

More broadly, prisons and jails are big business, a thriving industry, a cash cow for state and local governments.

There are masons, plumbers, carpenters, construction firms, and retailers who provide commissary items where a tiny bag of tuna fish cost up to $2.00, phone that charge exorbitant per minute rates for each call.

Parent of incarnated children have to send hundred of dollars to assure that they children are eating properly. This is an enormous burden on those, in many cases, struggling to survive as it is.

Where is all of this headed? Are my students, present and future, to be sacrificed on the altar of capitalism? Or will this nation find love and compassion for children who have sinned against God and man. Perhaps, in our compassion, we will find our own deliverance. Or are these children of a lesser God?

Having said that, what would I say to the bereaved family of a murder victim who continue to suffer in the aftermath? What if a member of my own family had fallen victim to one of them? World I still advocate benevolent reforms?

The answer is yes.

Once the pain subsides and clarity of mind returns, I would see that the system is not doing enough, neither for the children nor for the families or communities that spawned them.

A man once said, "A nation's greatness is measured by how it treats it women and children."

If this is true then, America still a ways to go before leaving its mark on the mantle of history.

What will it take to help these children, and in so doing help ourselves? It's going to take the bravery shown on Normandy Beach, the ingenuity that landed us on the moon, and the sacrifice displayed in the Marshal Plan.

But, more importantly, it's going to take people getting involved. If it is your choice to make a difference, start by becoming informed.

11 WE'RE DIFFERENT, BUT WE'RE THE SAME

For all of the problems race has caused the world, our differences are no more than skin deep. Genetically speaking, <u>race does not exist.</u> So much of the harm done in the world (war, slavery, torture and intolerance) is done in name of race, religion, and culture.

It is around these three principle categories that mankind has chosen to organize itself. But, to understand who we are, we have to look deep inside us. For inside us is a story waiting to be told, a story of sex, great adventure and survival.

Using the tools of science we have rendered open doors to our ancient past, doors that had formally been locked and its secret out of reach. However, genetic sciences now allow us to trace the journey of each and every person alive today.

Genealogy may allow most of us to sketch our ancestors back four or five generations, by no means a nominal feat. In contrast, DNA test tell a far deeper story, taking us back many thousands of generations. A simple swab of our cheek cells allows us access to a DNA history book, our own genetic document.

That document has been copied and passed down through the ions. No matter where we are from in the present or how different we may appear on the surface, following our genetic tree we all come from the same place.

In essence, we descended from a small group of Homo sapiens whose beginning stretches back 200,000 years. At some point they would leave Africa, giving raise to the present rendition of mankind. Ancient man may have started together, following diverging paths that led them to meet up with themselves, often not recognizing themselves.

We are different, but we're not

Humans are the most physically varied species on the planet because our ancestors were forced to adapt to different climates. Yet, looks can be deceiving. We are basically identical on the genetic level. Compare my DNA sequence to any other person and you'll find the two helixes 99.1 % identical.

So, whether your skin is black, white, brown, your eyes are blue, brown, or green, or whether you are big or small, minuscule genetic changes account for all of our differences. Significantly, scientist can now track DNA material that remains unchanged over eons of time.

My Y chromosome (and every other man's on earth) has been passed down from father to son for thousands of generations tracing back to one man about 60, 000 years ago. You heard me correct. As a timeline marker, the Pyramids of Giza were only constructed 5,000 years ago. Scientific Adam (African male home sapiens), as some geneticist like to call him, wasn't the only man back then, but his Y chromosome survived down through the ages. And, every guy alive today has a copy of his DNA.

For women like my wife and daughter, they are embodied with a mitochondria (special) cell structure that both men and women carry but only moms get to pass along. These cells trace back to one woman whose footprints go back 100,000 to 150,000 years. Scientific Eve then is the oldest root of our (human) family tree. Thus, Scientific Eve set the stage for us all, one baby at a time.

<u>African is where the journey began for everyone alive today.</u>

Plot the many amazing journeys out of Africa, and you can locate every single lineage in the world, albeit contained in a large pool of diverse cultures and races. This epic saga of twist and turns left many genetic markers, and these markers can be traced.

Most of us cling tightly to our collections of dusty photographs and deteriorating birth records that sometimes go back a hundred years. They often take us to faraway lands and strange and exotic places. But, by contract, our DNA markers may take us back over 6,000 generations to many lands to our ancient grandmothers (somewhere between eastern and southern Africa).

So, what are markers?

Random changes to the A, C, T, G markers (along the strand of the human genome) accumulate in our genetic code over time. These changes are called markers. They help to trace our ancestral journey.

A marker is a glimpse of person in the distant past. *If you share a marker you share an ancestor.* Remember that we are 99.1 % similar. To trace our ancestors, scientists have had to pour through the .1 % that is different.

These markers don't change the way you look or give you a disease or make you better that someone else, they're just necessary baggage that gets passed down through the generations.

Approximately, 200,000 years ago there began these random changes; G became T and so on. And early modern man began to pass the changes down.

Markers allow us to connect people through history, like a family tree. And, they can be used to date people because they crop up at a fairly regular rate. In essence, markers can be used as a clock to estimate when people lived. And because markers cluster they can even also act as a roadmap to tell us where our ancestors came from.

Geneticist study these lines of movement carefully, and there are hundreds of them.

Taken together they give us a timeline of human migration. Significantly, these genetic diversities or markers are more diverse in Africa than outside African. <u>This means that most of the changes took place there, proving that the human species originated in Africa.</u> Thus, the human species remained in African ¾ of our time or 140 thousand years before venturing out.

Climatic models indicate that life was good for Scientific Eve and her earliest descendents. They were blessed with flowing rivers and lust savannas. Food was plentiful. But, over the centuries that comfortable existence was interrupted. Climatic shift maybe the cause of their leaving and of their branching out.

One hundred and fifty years ago our genetic code split into two of the first branch of our family tree, joining up at the base of the tree. It was around this time that changes in the earth's orbit caused a climate shift; Africa became blistering dry and dessert-like, almost no rain fell for thousands of years.

The ecological phenomenon drove a wedge between populations and placed man on the brink of annihilation with man hanging on by a thread. Mankind had become an endangered species.

Nevertheless, our genetic cousins of thousands of years ago survived by their wit and powers of observation. They were forced to become more knowledgeable (smarter), developing essential skills in order to survive. It was survival of the fittest, with new tools cropping up and new lineages spreading out. Thus, mankind survived perhaps the toughest period in our history and came booming back.

However, this population crunch may have resulted in the scarcity that would eventually lead them to look elsewhere for sustenance. And in so doing, they took steps that would change the world forever. They left Africa behind.

Where by traveling over land or bodies of water, early man found a way to bridge the divide.

Some evidence indicates that they followed a northern route across the Sahara and then across the Sinai into the Middle East. But most anthropologists think that it was the southern tip of the Red Sea (a mere 17 miles from Africa to the Arabian Peninsula) where they crossed. Regardless, 60,000 years ago genetic markers indicate they left.

Reaching the Arabian Peninsula, their expert fishing skills served them well. Foraging the shoreline and rivers, they traveled through to Iran and then Pakistan and all the way to Asia. Upon reaching mainland Asia, they found the water exceedingly low, making it possible for the Africans to reach the distance Java and other islands of the South Pacific.

With the islands linked in such a fashion, these African groups were able to walk to Indonesia and Australia almost without getting their feet wet. Keep in mind that moving in small ingredients over long periods of time resulted in great dist*ances being reached. Aborigines had to cope with 45 miles of open water. Deliberately or blown off course they reached Australia 45,000 years ago.*

Here would be a good time to mention the earlier exits by the Homo erectus and Neanderthals from African, beating the Home sapiens by roughly 18, 000 thousand years. The groups may have mingled at some point, but the former groups did eventually die out.

But, let's get back to Asia and the islands of Oceania. Even today the evidence is clear. The oldest indigenous people of the Philippines tell the story. Living in isolation from other groups on the Island, their physical and genetic traits are strikingly similar (practical identical) to groups in eastern Africa.

In contrast to the groups that traveled the island route, other groups (clusters) journeyed across the great northern land mass of Asia. Here as in Oceania, the surroundings were gradually shaping their adaptations (phenotype) through natural selection. It may have only taken a few thousand years to bring about significant transformations, with groups mixing and matching everywhere that they went.

The recession of the ice age allowed Africa to flourish again and prompted the second migratory wave out of Africa. Nomads of the desert tell us a story of the first inhabitants of the Sahara. There Y chromosome samples indicate that people returned to Africa when new opportunities presented themselves (with grassland and lakes that had spread north of the continent).

The first major establishment in India was about 35,000 years ago, as they trekked across northern Asia. According to genetic markers, 50% of all European men followed the Himalayas into India and central Asia, which may have been an oasis of grasslands at the time.

Forty- thousand years ago these grasslands were the sources of a great deal of mixing, high mountain peaks provided water and the land supported vital vegetation. As the climate once again shifted (a second Ice Age, they began to invent techniques for making warm clothing, fashioning weapons, and food preparation. It was these cultural and technological events that allowed them to survive.

In tropical environments man needed protection from the sun. In colder climate the sun was less of a threat 40,000 years ago. And, as sunlight was hard to come by, people (Grimaldi man and the first Europeans) began to lose certain elements of their pigmentation and began lightening up.

Dark skin is a natural sun block(melanin being essential to man's survival) , but Vitamin D allowing skin was necessary for essential bone-building. In the tundra of Central Asia sunlight was scarce and dark skin a liability as people needed to let in all the sunlight they possibly could in order to survive. Eye color and hair texture are some other adaption that took place.

Like our other physical variations, changes in our genetic code, responsible for our shades of color, were miniscule. A few changes out of the few billion letters in the human genome formed the foundation of humanities' entire notion of race.

Without these changes people may not have survived to populate the rest of the world. And during this same period, the ice receded and the grasslands radiated outward deeper into the Asian steppe. Our genetics history further shows that other groups moved toward Western Europe, following the grassland to the North Sea and the Atlantic Ocean. Throughout these massive but incremental movements, mixing of genetic clusters continued.

Eleven thousand years ago groups moved into North America and spread down to the tip of South America. In a mere 15,000 years, they had reached Caribbean Islands like Puerto Rico.

But the second Ice Age was well on its way to retreating .The land mass binding North America and Russia vanished into the sea, cutting off the group from the rest of humanity until Columbus (or perhaps the Norseman or builders of the Omec heads)

Slavery blurred of bloodlines where black men today carry genetic markers of Europeans. In addition, traits that have existed for generations are continuing to fall as people from all walks of life come together through unparalleled global migration, a mega family reunion. 60, 000 years ago there was but one race, one lineage, one mankind.

While race is (in the genetic sense) superficial, it remains the single more destructive concept devised by man. So, are people ready to accept the reality of one human family?   The answer is no. People will continue to work hard to keep their roots alive. But, that may not be a bad thing as long as racial identity is kept in perspective.

I have purposefully, and with great difficulty, left my own anthropological, ideological and political interpretations out of this piece. I leave that to the reader. Some will take great offense to the role of Africa in man's creation or the origin of the human race, while other may fine hope for a better world with the realization and reality of our common past.

No matter your viewpoint, we are different, but we're not.

12 GOD, MAN, AND CREATION

I've passed beyond this world and experienced worlds greater in number than all the grains of sand on all the beaches of the earth. I have bathed in the truth of the living waters, found eternity in the moment and seen the universe in a grain of sand. All imaged boundaries faded in to a forgotten dream. Through the eternal spirit, the totality of creation has been revealed to me.

I was fed Nirvana from the open hand of the Great Buddha, awoke to the dawn of the Christ Spirit, bowed in prayer with the Prophet Mohammed at an eternal sunset, meditated in the garden of creation beside Lao Tzu, and was guided through the Great Hall of Souls by Upanishads, Keeper of the collective consciousness of man.

Freed of all earthly chains, my soul transcended.

Beyond the veil of the material world laid worlds of freely interpenetrating spectrums of light energy emanating from a vibratory essence. Starting with a creative pulsation of divine volition, man begins his journey into being. Down through the spiritual, astral and material planes he descends. This emanation of light grows dimmer and dimmer as the soul descends to the low levels of consciousness.

Finally, the eternal substance becomes manifest in earthly clothing.

Man's manifestation on the material plain is part of the divine process of creation, where life acts upon life to eternally perpetuate itself. All becoming all. Essence preceding existence. The One becomes the many without losing any part of itself. The Whole is present in all of it parts as the part is present in the Whole. As the light of creation resides in man, man possesses a gushing fountain of unconditional potentiality.

Sadly, in the lower conscious state, he remembers not his wholeness, his oneness with all of creation. Instead, he remained trapped by the very tools he uses to view the world. His logical mind aided by the sensory organs spits his reality, casting him afloat in the waters of life.

Most souls are held under the siren's lure of the five senses. The enlightened; however, see with mystical eyes, hear with ears born of the immaterial, and feel textures of countless variety. Their awareness encompasses the astral side of the five senses as well as a sixth and seventh senses. The sixth-sense exists as intuition and the seventh as thought transfer. Everyone has these synchronistic experiences at one time or another, but lacking knowledge of the cosmic laws of the universe, they brush them off as coincidences or unexplainable phenomena.

Some heightened souls, while on earth, cultivate their spiritual nature, surpassing the use of the five senses to achieve extraordinary vision. These souls may either use their powers for the good of the planet or for selfish enterprises thus inviting calamity and loss of power. By giving in to their bestial nature, these few retard humanity's spiritual restoration.

They act as false prophets (betraying God and man) steering humanity away from there light of truth. Their world is flooded with negative thought-forms that vibrate at base frequencies. Humanity is then held in the grips of perpetual slumber. He is unable to awaken to the eternal sunrise and his rightful place in the universal order.

These thought-forms fasten man's linear perception of the past, present, and future. His time machine provides a spatial and temporal corridor that plays host to his object reality. At the center of his imaginary universe is his created self, his ego self.

In the ego dominated world, man's lower nature rules supreme. Believing that he exist as a part of yet apart from all of creation, man ignores his immortality and wages all out war against what he perceives to be a treat to his continued existence.

The ego nature is exclusively concerned with the finite world, a world of objectives. The ego's council is false. It whispers words of deception in man's ear as he sleeps. He assures man that the dream is reality and reality is but a dream. The words describe a world of boundaries and separation. From the initial separation of man and divinity, a myriad of boundaries emerge to imprison him. The human personality then governed by categories of limitation beginning with the supposed separation of matter and energy.

Earth's scientist are beginning discover what mystic sages have known for eons. Matter and energy are two different sides of the same coin. At the very essence, this dichotomy (as with all others) is the Great Void discernible in the physical robes of duality and multiplicity.

Here lays the ontological keys to the celestial doors of divinity. Unlocking the door, an ever existing and ever reaching sea of pure energy that is existence is revealed. Man's oneness with all of existence is discovered. With this illumination comes the power to cure the sick, transformed smoke to stone, or transcend the time-space continuum. All things are possible in this elevated state of consciousness.

Others cannot let go. They are held in the hellish grips of the demons of their own mind.

Not even the fellowship of the Doves can reach them in these dark, putrid dungeons of the ego-mind's creation. They may be reincarnated but, only to begin again below evolutionary stage of a man. That soul will have to circumambulate up through the sublevels of the material plane.

Life acting upon life creating a cosmic helix spiral.

The helix is composed of a cosmic substance emulating from the living intelligence in the hologramic medium of sub-atomic particles. This atomic singularity is the source of all matter, including the body of man, and is the buttress of objective reality.

Souls that have suffered great guilt or pain on earth may relive those experiences, and thus reviving those emotions. Sorrow and self-loathing may descend upon those who have taken a life or inflected great pain on others. He or she has to learn to let go of the terrible wrongs. Before they can ascend to higher levels within the astral plane, they have to forgive others as well as themselves.

These thoughts weigh heavy on the soul, and cause it to resonate at a lower frequency. Reincarnation may be the only way for them to work through and overcome the thoughts of pain or suffering that impedes their progression. Some may live out several lives before accomplishing them.

While the astral plane is mutable and altered by the power of thought, the soul cannot be fooled like the mind, which may be tricked into mistaking a lie for the truth. One by one the illusions of sins or mistakes and the self-condemnation that surely follows, must be brought into light of truth. There they are banished forever from all planes of existence. On the higher sub-levels of the astral plane, thoughts flow in melodious accord with the rhythm of creation. The eyes of the soul enjoy misty waterfalls, dazzling sunrises, placid gardens and wondrous mountains vistas.

To speed their journey to the phases beyond the astral plane, some higher souls serve other souls who are confined by their thoughts to grosser levels. When the angels of light drives out the last vestiges of darkness, these souls of a lower plane will transcend into the causal plane consisting of pure consciousness.

Awaiting them on the casual plane is still subtler energy levels where even thoughts and memories are no longer needed. The soul may choose to exist as an eternal thought, an eternal scintillation of light from the ethereal Sun, or enter the dreamless sleep of Avatar. By letting go of ideation, the soul is freed from the last feelings of insufficiency, limitation, and finitude. Letting go of the memories of mortality, the soul is free to exist as a divine thought even after dissolution.

Oceans of light envelope the soul. All desires and cravings are gone, because the objects of all one's fears are dissolved. The illusions that accompany finite thoughts are shattered and dispelled from the boundless province of the soul.

Beyond the initial stages of the casual plain are the seven eternities. Mother, beyond this man cannot conceptualize or visualize. It is beyond his imagination or speculation. All that I can tell you is the living presence assures that everyone achieves happiness in the end and all creation works to that end.

13 MY MIS-EDUCATION

Sitting in the career development university library, I came to the stark realization that there were precious few jobs in the market for those with a B.A. in Political Science. Law school was the expected path. Though, a civil service career remained an option if you didn't mind starting at the bottom. Though most required the passing of exams which terrified me. I even looked in to the possibility of a career in the military. But, with my knee operation, there was no way I could survive boot camp.

I even applied for a job with the FBI and CIA, but I was never contacted for an interview. It came as no surprise to me though. While I was on the President's list my senior year, my GPA was less than impressive. And, what made me think that they would be interested in a black graduate with a "C" average and no other outstanding qualifications.

There was the chance that they wanted some Black Nationalist or Black Muslim organization infiltrated. My intellectual indoctrination complete, I would have sold out my own people for chump change. Would I have really done that? No doubt. Tony Brown, a renowned black journalist, once said: "it is impossible to send a black man to a white university and get black man back."

He was right in my case, if ever I was black. Instead of developing a broad and critical intellect, I managed a narrow and pedantic mindset. By the time my brainwashing (Eurocentric worldview) was complete, I was more estranged from myself (Afrocentric self) than at any time in my short life.

It was William Yeats who said:"Education is not the filling of a mind, but the lighting of a fire."

The fire that I brought with me had been extinguished, doused by well constructed lies, crafty distortions, and deliberate omissions. The thought police had done a thorough job in training me to think what I was told to think. What they called education was simply the exaltation of white culture.

Had I received a single grain of "education", I would have left school a devoted warrior, prepared to do battle against apartheid, the institutional extermination of black babies, the genocidal spread of heart disease among black males, the economic underdevelopment of the black Diaspora (worldwide), the exploitation of black minds by the white media, the wholesale imprisonment of black men, the erasing of black achievement from the pages of history, the commercial plundering of black culture (for its music, its dress, its style and its ideas), and the endless rape of Mother Africa.

So, it wasn't until I had earned and received a Bachelor's Degree and two Master Degrees that my real education begun. When did yours begin? Or has it?

Knowledge is Power

ABOUT THE AUTHOR

JAMES HALL was born and raised in Harlem, USA. He has been in education for the past 30 years. Mr. Hall earned a B.A. in Political Science from New York State University at Potsdam, a M.A. in Urban Studies from Long Island University, and a M.S. in General Sciences from New York City College. He has received numerous teaching awards, Science Fellowship Awards, and has written from the National Historical Society. He currently resides in Baltimore, Maryland.

James A. Hall